Just-in-Time Teaching

New Pedagogies and Practices for Teaching in Higher Education series

In the same series:

Blended Learning
Across the Disciplines, Across the Academy
Edited by Francine S. Glazer

Cooperative Learning in Higher Education
Across the Disciplines, Across the Academy
Edited by Barbara J. Millis

Published in Association with The National Teaching and Learning Forum

Just-in-Time Teaching

Across the Disciplines, Across the Academy

Edited by Scott P. Simkins *and* Mark H. Maier

Foreword By James Rhem

Published in Association with The National Teaching and Learning Forum

STERLING, VIRGINIA

Published by Stylus Publishing, LLC
22883 Quicksilver Drive
Sterling, Virginia 20166-2102

Library of Congress Cataloging-in-Publication-Data

Just-in-time teaching : across the disciplines, across the academy / edited by Scott Simkins and Mark H. Maier ; foreword by James Rhem.
    p. cm. — (New pedagogies and practices for teaching in higher education)
  Includes index.
  ISBN 978-1-57922-292-5 (cloth : alk. paper) —
  ISBN 978-1-57922-293-2 (pbk. : alk. paper)
  1. College teaching.
  LB2331.J78 2010
  378.1'25—dc22   2009026411

13-digit ISBN: 978-1-57922-292-5 (cloth)
13-digit ISBN: 978-1-57922-293-2 (paper)

Printed in the United States of America

All first editions printed on acid free paper
that meets the American National Standards Institute
Z39-48 Standard.

Bulk Purchases

Quantity discounts are available for use in workshops and for staff development.
Call 1-800-232-0223

First Edition, 2010

10 9 8 7 6 5 4 3 2 1

ACKNOWLEDGMENTS

We are grateful to be given the opportunity to bring together such a talented group of authors to share the benefits of Just-in-Time Teaching (JiTT) across the disciplines and across the academy. For that opportunity we thank James Rhem and Susan Slesinger, who guided the development not only of this book, but also the "New Pedagogies and Practices for Teaching in Higher Education" series. This series will be a valuable addition for instructors looking for ideas on how to improve student learning in their classes.

In addition, we are indebted to the original developers of JiTT, who over a decade ago began thinking carefully about how to more effectively engage physics students in the learning process. Little did they know that this pedagogy would be adopted and adapted by instructors not only in the physical and natural sciences, but also in the social sciences and the humanities. Our chapter authors represent this entire spectrum and are leaders in extending the use of this pedagogical innovation. We're excited to showcase the fruits of their many years of pedagogical research and practice.

Much of the work developing Just-in-Time Teaching has been supported by the National Science Foundation, in particular through its Course, Curriculum, and Laboratory Improvement (CCLI) Program. We thank the NSF for its ongoing support not only of JiTT, but also a growing collection of effective pedagogical innovations originally developed for the science, technology, engineering, and math (STEM) fields. Many of these innovations have had an important impact on teaching and learning outside of the disciplines in which they originated.

Finally, we have to say a special thank you to our wives, Jan Simkins and Anne Schiller, for their ongoing support of our work. Their patience, love, and encouragement are important sources of inspiration and joy for us. We couldn't do this work without them.

S. P. S. and M. H. M.

Contents

Foreword

James Rhem

Not that long ago, the word "pedagogy" didn't occur very often in faculty conversations about teaching. Today, one hears it frequently. Without putting too much weight on the prominence of a single word, subtle shifts in discourse, in vocabulary, often do mark significant shifts in thinking, and faculty thinking about teaching has changed over the last several decades. Faculty have always wanted to teach well, wanted their students to learn and succeed, but for a very long time faculty have taught as they were taught; for the students who were like them in temperament and intelligence, the approach worked well enough. When only a highly filtered population of students sought higher education, the need to look beyond those approaches to teaching lay dormant. When a much larger and more diverse population began enrolling, the limits of traditional teaching emerged more sharply.

At the same time, intelligence itself became a more deeply understood phenomenon. Recognition of multiple kinds of intelligence—visual, auditory, kinesthetic, etc.—found wide acceptance, as did different styles of learning even within those different kinds of intelligence (as measured, for example, by the Myers-Briggs Type Indicator (MBTI) developed by Katharine Cooks Briggs and Isabel Myers Briggs). Efforts to build ever more effective "thinking machines," that is to say, computers, through artificial intelligence sharpened understanding of how information needed to be processed in order for it to be assembled and utilized effectively. The seminal article, "Cognitive Apprenticeship: Teaching the Craft of Reading, Writing and Mathematics" was one by-product of this research, and one instructive aspect of this work lay in how it looked back to accumulated wisdom to lay its foundations for moving forward. Public schools had long dealt with large, diverse populations rather than highly filtered ones. Teachers there understood "scaffolding," "wait time," and "chunking" in conscious ways that were new to teachers at more advanced levels in education. Now, many of these terms, and more importantly these conscious and deliberate ways of thinking about teaching, have become commonplace in higher education.

Even more recently all this work has found support and expansion in the findings of neurobiological research into the human brain and how it operates, and in the study of groups and how they operate.

If renewed attention to teaching in higher education began as something of a "fix-it" shop approach aimed at helping individual faculty having problems with their teaching, it didn't stay that way very long. As Gaff and Simpson detail in their history of faculty development in the United States, pressure from the burgeoning "baby boom" population brought the whole business of university teaching up for reconsideration. What was relevance? What were appropriate educational goals, and what were the most effective means of meeting them? Traditionally, the primary expectation of faculty was that they remain current in their fields of expertise. Now, a whole new set of still forming expectations began to spring up on campuses all over the country.

Change often fails to come easily and smoothly. Generational and social conflicts, together with passionate political conflicts centering on the unpopular war in Vietnam may have fueled the pressure for changes in teaching while making them more conflict-ridden than they needed to be.It is important to repeat: faculty have always wanted to teach well and have their students succeed. As the clouds of conflict from those decades have passed, the intellectual fruits have remained and grown. Some ascribe credit for change in faculty attitudes toward teaching to the social pressures of those decades. Whatever truth lies in that ascription, it seems equally clear that faculty's innate intellectual curiosity and eagerness to succeed in their life's work deserve as much credit, certainly for today's faculty interest in improved teaching.

Faculty face a challenge in embracing new understandings of effective teaching not unlike the challenge of any population of diverse intelligences in learning and applying new information. Some understanding emerging in the 1980s (in which much of the new thinking on teaching and learning began to appear) has cross-disciplinary, universal applicability, for example, the "Seven Principles of Good Practice in Higher Education" by Chickering and Gamson. But just as diverse people learn in diverse ways, diverse faculty will apply even universal principles in different ways, becaise both personalities and disciplinary cultures vary. Perhaps that is why many pedagogical insights into effective teaching have not aggregated into one universal, best way to teach. Instead the forward moving inquiry into effective teaching has spawned a variety of pedagogical approaches, each with strengths appropriate to particular teaching styles and situations.

While faculty today have greater curiosity about new understandings of effective ways to teach, they remain as cautious as anyone else about change. If they teach biology, they wonder how a particular approach might play out in teaching biology rather than how it works in teaching English literature. If they teach English literature, they may wonder if problem-based teaching (an approach highly effective in the sciences) has anything to offer their teaching and if anyone in their discipline has tried it. Every new idea requires translation and receives it in the hands of the next person to take it up and apply it in their work. And this is as it should be. Thus, this series of books strives to give faculty examples of new approaches to teaching as they are being applied in a representative sample of academic disciplines. In that, it extends the basic idea of *The National Teaching and Learning FORUM*. For roughly 20 years, the central goal of *FORUM* has been to offer faculty ideas in contexts; that is to say, to present them enough theory so that whatever idea about teaching and learning being discussed makes sense intellectually, but then to present that idea in an applied context. From this combination faculty can see how an approach might fit in their own practice. Faculty do not need formulae, they need only to see ideas in contexts. They'll take it from there. And so our series of books offers faculty a multipaned window into a variety of nontraditional pedagogical approaches now being applied with success in different disciplines in higher education. Faculty will look in and find something of value for their own teaching. As I've said and believe with all my heart, faculty have always wanted to teach well and see their students succeed.

—James Rhem,
Executive Editor,
The National Teaching and Learning FORUM

Editors' Preface

Just-in-Time Teaching Across the Disciplines

Scott P. Simkins and Mark H. Maier

After participating in a Just-in-Time Teaching (JiTT) workshop in the late 1990s led by Gregor Novak and Evelyn Patterson—the early developers of this pedagogical practice—we changed the way we taught. Inspired by their results, we introduced JiTT into our economics courses, requiring students to answer questions related to upcoming class material a few hours before class using an online course management system. The results were positive and immediate. Students came to class better prepared and reported that the JiTT exercises helped to focus and organize their out-of-class studying. In addition, students' responses to JiTT questions made gaps in their learning visible to us prior to class. This knowledge allowed us to create classroom activities that directly addressed those learning gaps while the material was still fresh in students' minds—hence the label "just in time"—leading to improved learning. We were hooked.

One of our spouses teased us by saying that we had simply "reinvented homework." Indeed, one advantage of JiTT is that it encourages students to read course-related material before class, spreading their work more evenly over the semester, often a significant step for students who believe that it is better to wait for the instructor to explain the course material. However, JiTT questions differ from traditional homework problems, which often involve simple applications of course concepts. Our JiTT questions are designed not only to build cognitive skills, but also to help students confront misconceptions, make connections to previous knowledge, and develop metacognitive thinking practices. As a result our students not only spend more time on course concepts and ideas, but they also read the textbook in ways that resulted in more effective and deeper learning.

JiTT also changed the way we conducted our classes. We post selected student JiTT responses (anonymously) on a screen in the front of the classroom at the start of class to introduce the day's content and implement small group activities; these activities were based on learning gaps identified by those responses as a jumping-off point for the class. We have found that starting the class with students' work dramatically changes the classroom learning environment, creating greater student engagement and participation. Students are more involved in the class when they work with authentic examples generated by their peers, and we are better attuned to the prior knowledge, misunderstandings, and attitudes that students bring to class.

This book demonstrates that we are not alone in our experience. JiTT has broad appeal across the academy, as instructors in disciplines ranging from physics to the humanities have found JiTT to be effective in promoting student learning. In order to appeal to this wide range of instructors, we have organized this book in two sections, providing general and discipline-centric views of JiTT pedagogy. Both will provide valuable insights on how to get started with JiTT in your own classes. Part I provides a broad overview of JiTT, introducing the pedagogy and exploring various dimensions of its use without regard to discipline. It begins with "Getting Started with JiTT" by Gregor Novak and Evelyn Patterson, who, along with fellow-physicists Andy Gavrin and Wolfgang Christian, developed the JiTT approach. Subsequent chapters in Part I demonstrate JiTT's growth and sophistication over the last decade. Mary Elizabeth Camp, Joan Middendorf, and Carol Subiño Sullivan (chapter 2) describe the importance of student motivation in successfully implementing JiTT and offer suggestions on how to effectively implement JiTT to maximize its impact on student learning. Eric Mazur and Jessica Watkins (chapter 3) explore the connection between JiTT and peer instruction, a highly successful in-class pedagogy promoting student-student interaction that can be used in both small and large classes. Our own chapter 4 rounds out the first section of the book and further explores the use of JiTT in combination with other pedagogical innovations, including context-rich problems, cooperative learning, and classroom experiments.

Part II of the book demonstrates JiTT's remarkable cross-disciplinary impact. Initially developed as a physics education initiative (Andy Gavrin, chapter 7), JiTT has been adapted in biology (Kathleen Marrs, chapter 5), the geosciences (Laura Guertin, chapter 6), economics (Scott Simkins and Mark Maier, chapter 8), history (David Pace and Joan Middendorf, chapter 9), and the humanities (Claude Cookman, chapter 10).

These chapters illustrate JiTT's role in promoting the effective teaching of discipline-specific concepts, principles, and practices, what Lee Shulman, former president of the Carnegie Foundation for the Advancement of Teaching, has termed *pedagogical content knowledge:* "the blending of content and pedagogy into an understanding of how particular topics, problems, and issues are organized, represented, and adapted to the diverse interests and abilities of learners and presented for instruction." (Shulman, 1987, p. 8) Although the specific implementation of JiTT varies across these chapters, the core element of JiTT pedagogy remains constant, in particular the interplay of preclass responses to JiTT questions and use of those responses to inform and direct in-class activities "just in time." As a result we expect that all instructors will find these chapters useful, even those outside their own discipline. For us, each chapter has proved a rich mine of ideas that we could adapt for our own discipline, offering us novel contexts for JiTT questions, creative in-class activities, and helpful advice about student motivation and student learning. We encourage readers of this book to similarly explore across disciplinary boundaries to find new ideas about how JiTT might be adapted in your own classes.

A few words on language. "Just in time" may bring to mind a business model assembly line that seeks to minimize the costs of learning. In fact, JiTT pedagogy does just the opposite, helping students to view learning as a process that takes time and introspection rather than memorization of chunks of material the night before a test. Similarly, for instructors, the JiTT approach suggests that the classroom is not an assembly line, but instead a learning environment that needs to be adjusted to what students know and bring to the classroom. For both students and teachers, JiTT requires rethinking the teaching and learning process. It is not simply an add-on to a course or a way to keep students busy out of class. To be successful, JiTT requires a change in *how* teaching and learning is done. The reward for this transformation is that students and instructors are better synchronized in their expectations about what it takes to learn new concepts at a deep level. As a result, both teaching and learning improve.

JiTT practitioners vary in the language they use to describe this pedagogy to students, distinctions that vary by discipline or course. JiTT questions answered by students before class frequently are called "warm-ups," "thinking about the readings," or, in the case of the U.S. Air Force Academy, "pre-flights." To reduce confusion for the reader, in this book we have chosen to use the terms "JiTT questions" or "JiTT exercise" (or simply, JiTTs) for all types of questions posed before class.[1] Of course, this does not preclude you from creating and using names for these exercises that are more relevant to your own course, institution, or discipline, or that are likely to increase student interest. Whatever works best for you, use it!

Throughout the chapters in this book you will note a number of common themes that undergird JiTT's success in the classroom, regardless of discipline. Foremost among these are the following:

(1) *The importance of structure.* Students use JiTT more effectively if its purpose is explained clearly in advance, noting the importance of regular pre-class assignments to systematically build cognitive and metacognitive skills using, for example, Bloom's (1956) taxonomy and the learning principles of *How People Learn* (Bransford, Brown, and Cocking, 2000) as guides. To be successful, JiTT exercises should be linked to important course learning outcomes and integrated into the class in an intentional manner.

(2) *The importance of flexibility.* As this volume makes clear, JiTT is readily adaptable across a wide spectrum of disciplines and can be used in conjunction with a large number of in-class teaching practices. In addition, we have found that instructor use of JiTT varies over time. The contributors to this book are quite forthcoming about errors they made when they first adopted JiTT pedagogy [see, in particular Camp, Middendorf, and Sullivan (Chapter 2) and Cookman (Chapter 10)]. We, too, have changed our JiTTs over time, for example varying types of questions to increase relevance and avoid student burn-out. JiTT is flexible enough to adapt to a wide range of teaching styles, learning environments, courses, disciplines, and institutions.

(3) *The importance of feedback and formative assessment.* Every author in this volume points to the benefit of the frequent and immediate feedback that JiTT offers to students. By showing JiTT responses in class and using them to direct in-class activities, students get regular feedback about learning gaps - information that can be used to focus and adjust their studying in time for more high-stakes evaluations such as exams, reports, or research papers.

(4) *The importance of student-centeredness.* Follow-up use of students' JiTT responses in the classroom means that class content, whether it be a traditional lecture or a small group activity, will be based on what students know (or don't know). In this way, instructors using JiTT maintain control over class content but have greater knowledge about what particular learning needs students have and how to address them. JiTT not only shows students that instructors care about their learning but also helps instructors intentionally transform the classroom learning environment in ways that are most beneficial to that learning.

(5) *The importance of research on learning.* Nearly every chapter refers to research on learning, independent of the discipline under discussion, including references to Arons (1979), Bloom (1956), Chickering and Gamson (1987), and most notably Bransford, Brown, and Cocking's *How People Learn* (2000). Grounding JiTT pedagogy in research on learning ensures that

pedagogical practice aligns with what we currently understand about how students learn and leads to effective classroom teaching.

(6) *The importance of building metacognitive skills.* A critical, but often overlooked element in effective teaching is the importance of developing students' ability to think about their own learning. JiTT is a useful tool for integrating reflective learning practices that help students understand what they know, what they don't know, and how to close the gap between the two. A common question on JiTT exercises is the following: After completing this exercise, what concepts or ideas are still unclear and why? In addition to helping students reflect on their own understanding of course material, this type of question also provides the instructor with a valuable window on student learning, which in turn can be used to inform in-class teaching and learning.

(7) *The importance of making student thinking visible.* JiTT exercises help to uncover student misconceptions that would otherwise remain hidden and often retard learning. As Bransford, Brown, and Cocking (2000) note, a critical element in effective teaching is directly addressing learning gaps that arise from students' misconceptions. Traditional lecture methods do not probe for this kind of information and as a result, instructors are often surprised when students fail to "learn" what they have been teaching. JiTT helps make students' thinking processes visible—providing an "intellectual footprint"—while there is time to address misconceptions that have been identified.

We have many individuals to thank for their assistance in bringing this volume to life. First and foremost, we appreciate the hard work and patience of the chapter authors, who have implemented JiTT in their own classrooms for many years and have been at the forefront of research on JiTT pedagogy. Without their work this volume would not have been possible. Their efforts have paid off in what we believe will be a substantial contribution to the pedagogical literature in their own disciplines as well as to a growing cross-disciplinary conversation on teaching and learning.

We are indebted, of course, to the original JiTT developers, Gregor Novak, Evelyn Patterson, Andrew Gavrin, and Wolfgang Christian (1999). These generous physics educators not only introduced us to JiTT, but have also continued to inspire us in our own work in this area over the years. We especially want to thank Gregor Novak, who assisted us in the initial development of this volume, in addition to writing the opening chapter with Evelyn Patterson.

Finally, we thank the National Science Foundation (NSF) for its support of JiTT, including funding the research that got JiTT off the ground in physics (DUE 9752365) and allowed these physics educators to promote the approach across the academy (for example, in chemistry, biology, and mathematics courses; DUE 9981111), including the workshops that first introduced us to JiTT. Subsequently, NSF supported the development of the JiTT Digital Library (DUE 0333646) and our own work adapting JiTT in economics (DUE 0088303) and exploring the connections between economics education and STEM-based pedagogical innovations such as JiTT (DUE 0411037). Our most recent NSF grant (DUE 0817382) is being used to create an economics pedagogic portal, "Starting Point: Teaching and Learning Economics," (http://serc.carleton.edu/econ/index.html) in conjunction with the Science Education Resource Center (SERC) at Carleton College. This project includes updating SERC's *Pedagogy in Action* module on Just-in-Time Teaching (http://serc.carleton.edu/sp/library/justintime/index.html) and developing a library of economics-related JiTT teaching examples, as well as a mechanism for sharing examples that illustrate the use of JiTT within and across disciplines.

We hope that after reading all or part of this book, you will be encouraged to experiment with JiTT in your own classroom, regardless of your discipline. We'd love to hear from you about your own experiences with this pedagogy and welcome questions and comments that you have about how to effectively integrate JiTT with your current teaching strategies. If you find JiTT useful in promoting your own students' learning, we encourage you to submit your own JiTT activities/exercises to the SERC *Pedagogy in Action* (http://serc.carleton.edu/sp/service/contribute.html) and the *JiTTDL* (http://jittdl.physics.iupui.edu/jit/DL/dsp_home.php) Web sites. Both are aimed at building an open "teaching commons" where successful teaching strategies are shared with other instructors across a wide variety of disciplines. We look forward to your contributions to this ever-growing community of JiTT practitioners.

March 2009

Note

1. In addition, some instructors have developed "Good Fors," in which students explore how course concepts apply to important real life issues, following coverage of a chapter or unit (see, for example, Kathleen Marrs in chapter 5).

References

Arons, A. B. (1979). Some thoughts on reasoning capacities implicitly expected of college students. In J. Lochhead & J. Clement (Eds.), *Cognitive process instruction: Research on teaching and learning skills* (pp. 209–215). Philadelphia, PA: Franklin Inst. Press.

Bloom, B. S. (1956). *Taxonomy of educational objectives, handbook I: The cognitive domain.* New York: David McKay Co.

Bransford, J. D., Brown, A. L., & Cocking, R. R. (Eds.). (2000). *How people learn: Brain, mind, experience, and school.* Washington, D.C.: National Academy Press.

Chickering, A. W., & Gamson, Z. F. (1987). Seven principles for good practice in undergraduate education. American Association for Higher Education Bulletin, 39 (7), 3–7.

Novak, G. M., Patterson, E. T., Gavrin, A. D., & Christian, W. (1999). *Just-in-time teaching: Blending active learning with web technology.* Upper Saddle River, NJ: Prentice Hall.

Shulman, L. S. (1987). Knowledge and teaching: Foundations of the new reform. Harvard Educational Review, 57 (1), 1–22.

Getting Started With Just-in-Time Teaching

1

An Introduction to Just-in-Time Teaching (JiTT)

Gregor Novak and Evelyn Patterson

If you are like most instructors who care deeply about their teaching, and more importantly about students' learning, you regularly reflect on how you can improve students' preparation for class, their intellectual curiosity, and their learning processes. In our experience, these issues are at the forefront of most faculty discussions about teaching and learning. Wouldn't you love to face a class that has done some preliminary reading, has thought about the subject, and has some questions for you? Don't we all wish for that? Well, it can happen. How? The following example provides some insight on how Just-in-Time Teaching (JiTT) can help.

AN EXAMPLE OF JUST-IN-TIME TEACHING

Consider the following scenario: You are preparing a lesson in an introductory-level course, in this case an introductory biology lesson on cloning. As you prepare your lesson you send your students to the course Web site and invite them to ponder the following three questions:

1. Dolly the sheep is a genetic twin, or clone, of a sheep that was born six years earlier than Dolly. Read the material for today. Does Dolly have parents? If so, who were her genetic parents? Is Dolly a "virgin birth"?
2. What is wrong with the thinking that if we were ever to clone a person, like Einstein, a brilliant physicist, we would end up with another brilliant physicist?
3. Can you think of a way that a person's genetic information might be used to discriminate against him/her for employment or insurance coverage? Give an example. How might employers or insurance companies obtain this knowledge?

After some thought and background reading, students post their answers to these questions online a few hours before class. A small sampling of these student responses (unedited) is provided below.

Question 1:

That's a hard question. She was cloned from the cell of a 6-year-old sheep. Dolly doesn't have what we would commonly think of as parents, but genetically her parents would be the same parents of the six year old sheep. So her parents would be the parents of the sheep she was cloned after.

Question 2:

We can't assume that a clone of Einstein would turn out just as brilliant and come up with as many, if not more brilliant theories because who and what a person is depends on the environment in which they live as well as the people they are surrounded with, influences in their lives as well as their genetics. Although it would be possible to recreate the genetic Einstein it would be impossible to recreate his entire childhood and all the influences in his life.

Question 3:

Although (new) laws are being reviewed/revised to take into consideration the "genetic factor" to curb unauthorized or improper use of personal medical records, most medically related processes require that you sign a release form—once signed we can probably kiss privacy goodbye. In the right/wrong hands, our SS# alone gives access to endless personal information, including medical records.

After reviewing all the student responses you organize them into common themes and select a representative sample to present anonymously at the beginning of the next class. In addition, you think carefully about how to weave the students' responses into your in-class lesson and instructional activities. To make the lesson as interactive as possible, you might develop in-class cooperative learning activities linked to students' responses or use the selected responses to generate full-class discussions. In turn, some of the thoughts that emerge during the class activities become the grist for future questions posted online for students to complete. Overall, through the sequencing of instructor-generated questions related to course topics, web submission of student responses, instructor use of the responses to guide in-class teaching and activities, and follow-up questions, the students and the instructor collectively guide the construction of new knowledge.

The scenario summarized describes the Just-in-Time Teaching (JiTT) pedagogy that Kathy Marrs (see chapter 5) uses throughout her introductory biology courses to promote student engagement and motivation. She, like many other JiTT adopters, has found that JiTT improves not only students' class preparation and study habits, but also their learning and course retention rates.

In the rest of this chapter we describe the structure of the JiTT technique and present ideas on how to get started with JiTT, including background information on how JiTT lessons are constructed, what typical JiTT exercises look like, and how they are followed up by classroom activities. The chapters that follow in this book illustrate JiTT's adaptability across disciplines, instructors, institution types, and course levels. Each chapter describes how JiTT has been used in a particular discipline or in a particular way to improve student learning.

BACKGROUND OF JUST-IN-TIME TEACHING

The Just-in-Time Teaching (JiTT) pedagogical strategy (Novak, Patterson, Gavrin, & Christian, 2000) was originally conceived in 1996 as part of an attempt to help nontraditional students improve their learning. Working with students at Indiana University Purdue University Indiana (an urban commuter campus) and at the U.S. Air Force Academy (a military campus), the original developers—Gregor Novak, Evelyn Patterson, and Andrew Gavrin—were striving to help students structure their out-of-class efforts and to get more out of precious in-class student-instructor face time. The advent of the Internet, with the ability to rapidly exchange information digitally at any time, allowed the students to do preparatory work between classes with ample time to reflect, and gave the instructor time to prepare lessons with timely student input—just in time for the next class period. Supported in part by a grant from the National Science Foundation in 1997, the three JiTT innovators began implementing this new teaching/learning strategy in their classrooms.[1] Five years later, well over 300 faculty members at more than 100 schools had adopted or adapted JiTT pedagogy for their own disciplines and classrooms, often through National Science Foundation-supported workshops promoting teaching innovations in science, technology, engineering, and math (STEM) fields.

As illustrated in the opening example, the key idea of JiTT pedagogy is to develop an intentional, direct linkage between in-class and out-of-class activities via preparatory web-based assignments—originally called "warmups" or "preflights" (with the obvious link to the U.S. Air Force Academy) but now commonly referred to as "JiTT exercises" or simply "JiTTs"—that generally require students to read, view, or do something and answer related questions.

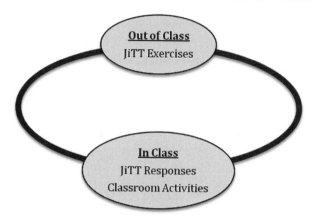

Figure 1.1 The JiTT Feedback Loop

The web-based materials, added as a pedagogical resource, act as a communication tool and organizer. Because much learning occurs outside the classroom, JiTT practitioners view their pedagogical strategy as a feedback loop between in-class and out-of-class experiences. Figure 1.1 illustrates this teaching/learning feedback loop.

The best JiTT exercises include short, thought-provoking questions that, when fully discussed, often have complex answers. Students are expected to develop answers to JiTT questions on their own, as far as they can, recognizing that the questions relate to material that has not yet been formally covered in the course. JiTT assignments are due a few hours before class time, giving the instructor enough time to incorporate the insights gained from student responses into the upcoming lesson. Work on the assignment continues in the classroom with the student-submitted responses playing an important part in the flow of the lesson. A sample of student responses is typically shown at the beginning of class and used as the basis for small-group or full-class discussions. In addition, classroom activities are developed to focus on student misunderstandings or difficulties uncovered in the student responses.

The JiTT classroom differs from traditional lecture in two significant ways. First, having completed the web assignment very recently, the students enter the classroom ready to participate actively in classroom activities. Second, students have a feeling of ownership because classroom activities are grounded in their own understanding of the relevant issues. Exactly how the classroom time is spent depends on a variety of issues such as class size, classroom facilities, and student and instructor personalities, but can include whole-class discussion, a demonstration, or cooperative learning exercises, and can be combined with other in-class teaching pedagogies such as peer instruction or inquiry-based learning (see chapters 3 and 4 for ideas on how to combine JiTT with other pedagogical innovations).

DEVELOPING EFFECTIVE JiTT QUESTIONS

The key to achieving success with JiTT lies in the development of effective JiTT questions. As is evident from the discipline-specific chapters in this book, the content and form of JiTT assignments vary significantly from discipline to discipline and from instructor to instructor, yet there are common key characteristics that characterize "good" JiTT questions. In general, effective JiTT questions

- yield a rich set of student responses for classroom discussion.
- encourage students to examine prior knowledge and experience.
- require an answer that cannot easily be looked up.
- require that students formulate a response, including the underlying concepts, in their own words.
- contain enough ambiguity to require the student to supply some additional information not explicitly given in the question (in particular, this feature enriches the subsequent classroom discussion).

It is useful to keep this list in mind as you develop your own JiTT questions. The characteristics can be organized into broad categories intentionally targeted by pre-instruction assignments. Examples of these are provided in the following "taxonomy" of learning objectives that underlie effective JiTT questions. Note that many of these can be directly linked to the growing literature in the learning sciences on how people learn (see, for example, Bransford, Brown, & Cocking, 2000). In addition, you can extend this list to include objectives that are specific to your own use or discipline.

Preparing for a Discussion of a Complex, Possibly Controversial Topic (Discussion Preparation). Classroom discussions typically require out-of-class reading and an in-depth knowledge of subject matter to be effective. Student participation will be enhanced if students come to class with informed responses that they are eager to defend. JiTT questions asking students to compare and contrast, evaluate, or provide evidence for ideas and concepts can be effective at promoting student engagement.

Getting beyond Memorization (Applying Concepts). In many subjects, learning definitions of technical terms and complex concepts leaves students uninterested in the subject matter or perplexed and confused about how to apply the concepts. In this situation, many students resort to novice learning strategies such as memorization, which disconnects the subject taught from conceptual understanding. In contrast, JiTT questions can create relevance, relating course concepts to student experience.

Reconstructing Ideas and Concepts (Personalizing Knowledge). It is very helpful to students if they are challenged to digest new ideas and concepts enough to be able to construct their own formulations of the information; that is, to fuse the two worlds into one and create new knowledge for themselves. "In your own words . . ." kinds of JiTT questions fall into this category.

Developing a Need to Know (Building Curiosity). Good JiTT questions are sufficiently captivating so that even weak students are interested in the answers and motivated to provide responses that do more than mechanically answer the question. It is then up to the instructor to build on this emerging motivation and sustain a lasting interest in the subject.

Reflecting on Their Learning (Developing Metacognition). This involves extending the understanding of concepts beyond simply learning the content. Ideally students would move from applying new concepts and information at their current level of understanding to a deeper synthesis between their current knowledge and the richer emerging knowledge. To do this, students have to be encouraged to critically monitor their own learning and take advantage of classroom sessions to check their progress.

Examples of effective JiTT questions are listed in Table 1.1. They are drawn from a variety of disciplines and illustrate many of the characteristics of "good" JiTT questions: those that are effective at uncovering misconceptions, promoting curiosity, and encouraging active student engagement in the learning process. For each of the questions, we have indicated which of the categories described above applies to the question.

In addition to illustrating examples of good JiTT questions, Table 1.1 also suggests a useful practice for developing effective JiTT questions: explicitly linking JiTT questions to key teaching and learning objectives in your course to ensure that JiTT questions are targeting and achieving intended student learning outcomes.

Table 1.1. A Sample of Effective JiTT Questions

1. **Introductory Biology:** What is the difference between a theory and a belief? You may want to look these terms up before answering. Be as specific as you can, and give an example of each. (discussion preparation, applying concepts)

2. **Logic:** The people of Finiteland only tell the truth on Sunday, Tuesday, and Thursday. Which day of the week is it if a person from Finiteland says, "I told the truth yesterday"? (building curiosity)

3. **Introductory Earth Science:** When reading or hearing news reports about dinosaur discoveries, what questions should you think about and ask yourself to evaluate the accuracy of the reports? (developing metacognition)

4. **Advanced Mechanics:** Your everyday experience, common sense, and math classes all suggest to you that the shortest distance between two points in two-dimensional space is a straight line (unless, of course, you want to consider a warped space-time continuum!). Please describe how you would go about proving that this is true, using the methods of variational calculus. Don't actually do this, but describe in English the procedure you would follow. Please be specific in your steps. (applying concepts)

5. **Chemistry:** Explain in simple terms how you solved warm-up #1. In particular, what questions did you ask yourself and what conclusions did you draw from the answers? (developing metacognition)

6. **Statistics:** Estimate the probability that a North American male is precisely six feet tall. (building curiosity, applying concepts)

7. **Introductory Physics:** Let's say you have a prescription for contact lenses of -2 diopters. If you accidentally get glasses (as opposed to contacts) made to the same strength, your prescription will be a bit off, and you won't be able to focus at infinity. Estimate how far you will be able to focus. (applying concepts, personalizing knowledge)

8. **Economics:** Imagine that you are a newspaper reporter assigned to write a story about the upcoming meeting of the Federal Open Market Committee. Make a list of three questions that you will want to ask. For each question, explain carefully why it is important and what answer you expect from the Committee. (applying concepts, personalizing knowledge, developing metacognition)

9. **Introductory Biology:** Allison is driving with her parents, Kate and Bob, when they get in a serious car accident. At the emergency room, her doctor (you) tells Allison that her mother is fine, but her father has lost a lot of blood and will need a blood transfusion. Allison volunteers to donate blood, and you tell her that her blood type is AB. Bob is type O. (a) Can Allison donate blood to Bob? Why or why not? (b) Allison, who is a biology student, begins to wonder if she is adopted. What would you tell her and why? (applying concepts, personalizing knowledge, building curiosity)

DOING JiTT: STEPS FOR EFFECTIVE IMPLEMENTATION

In this section, we take you through the steps of the Just-in-Time Teaching process from beginning to end, pointing out how to make effective use of this pedagogy in your classes. Note that we're necessarily taking a helicopter view of the process here—the remainder of the book will provide specific examples of how JiTT is used across the academy. Our purpose here is simply to provide you with general guidance on JiTT implementation based on our experience and that of colleagues who have shared their own suggestions with us over the years.

Preparing Students for JiTT

JiTT exercises require students to engage in a preliminary exploration of the topic for the upcoming lesson before the topic is covered in class. The exact task involved will depend greatly on the course subject and level, but experienced JiTT instructors construct JiTT exercises in such a way that students are led to build connections between the new material and previous knowledge. For many students, this is an unfamiliar task, especially if their previous educational experience has simply been one of accumulating information and replicating that information on quizzes and exams.

For most students, explanation of what is expected of them and how they will be rewarded for their effort is critical for JiTT success. This is particularly important because the focus of JiTT exercises is on the thinking processes of students prior to in-class coverage of a topic, not the ability to replicate exact knowledge (as is often the case on exams). With JiTT, students are expected to explore the upcoming lesson topic on their own and respond to the questions in the JiTT exercise, drawing on previous experience from their lives, prior coursework, information from the text, an article, a video, the results of a simulation, or some other activity. Articulating the status of their knowledge or thinking processes at this preliminary point helps the instructor conduct a meaningful interactive classroom discussion or activity, with extensive student participation. Students get credit for the preliminary exploratory work and their effort at connecting ideas, not for having mastered all the material.

Most JiTT practitioners have found it essential to give their students not only a clear idea of the structure of JiTT assignments, but also the purpose of this structure in promoting student learning. Students tend to view any assignment as a summative assessment, ultimately linked to the course grade, rather than an opportunity to practice critical thinking skills and achieve course, program, or institutional learning objectives. If JiTT is implemented in a class without a discussion of its educational purpose, many students will view JiTT as simply shifting the burden of teaching from the instructor to the student. To be most successful, students should understand that JiTT is a formative learning technique aimed at improving their learning process by providing frequent feedback to both students and instructors so that in-class interactions can be used most productively to focus on learning gaps and challenges that otherwise might go unseen until exams are graded. When the students perceive JiTT exercises as nonjudgmental diagnostic tools they become more willing to take risks and reveal the actual state of their knowledge.

Of course, there is no guarantee that even the most careful explanation will shake many students' belief that to teach means to tell and to learn means to pay attention and remember. Nevertheless, with an explicit discussion about the educational foundations of JiTT practices at the start of a course, many students begin to understand and appreciate the regular use of JiTT exercises, even though they may at times grow weary of the daily or weekly effort required. Informal student comments reveal that many of them appreciate the formative self-assessment that JiTT exercises provide.

Developing Effective JiTT Questions

As noted in the previous section, development of good JiTT questions is central to the effectiveness of JiTT pedagogy. It is important to keep in mind the educational objectives you have in mind when you sit down at the keyboard to draft the questions for a particular lesson topic. Is the primary purpose to simply prepare students for an in-class discussion? To challenge students to extend a concept beyond what is written in the textbook—for example, to apply, evaluate, or synthesize ideas? To motivate students to think about a particular concept by connecting a new idea to a real-life problem or life experience? To uncover student thought processes? To enhance students' ability to evaluate and monitor their own learning? As emphasized throughout this chapter, what you expect students to learn, and what you expect to learn from the students' responses, depends in an important way on the types of JiTT questions that you ask. Putting time and effort into the question-development phase of the JiTT process will pay large dividends for you in terms of student learning and the clarity and organization of your course material. The better that you can align JiTT questions with your course learning objectives and integrate student responses in the natural flow of the course, the less likely that students will view JiTT exercises as "add-ons" or "busy work," and the more likely that they will value your efforts as a teacher to respond to their learning needs.

In addition to concept or idea-related questions, JiTT exercises often include a question such as "After completing this exercise, what ideas are still unclear to you?" Responses to this type of question can be used to better understand what difficulties students are having in your classes that go beyond the specific JiTT questions being posed. An alternative is to include a space on the JiTT assignment web page for student comments related to the JiTT exercise. Often, these comments contain a treasure trove of helpful metacognitive observations. Given the opportunity, many students are very good at expressing their thought processes, which may not be captured in direct responses to JiTT questions. The comments can uncover misconceptions, bad study practices, background holes, and hidden anxieties, all of which hinder student learning. Intentionally and explicitly responding in class to common student difficulties disclosed in the JiTT responses builds a sense of joint teacher-student knowledge production that promotes continued participation in JiTT exercises and shared responsibility for the learning environment in the course.

Posting JiTT Questions and Setting Response Deadlines

It is important not only to be explicit with your students about the educational purposes of JiTT exercises but also to clearly lay out the process for successfully completing the exercises. Your syllabus should indicate where JiTT exercises can be found, how responses are to be submitted, and when the exercises are due. Following a consistent pattern—for example, requiring all JiTT responses to be submitted by 10 p.m. on the due date—is the best way to reduce student confusion and ensure success. You will have to determine what schedule works best for you and your students, but note that students often find the early morning (1–3 a.m.) hours the most convenient for them. Especially if you are new to JiTT, set your submission deadlines so that you have enough time to analyze the responses prior to class without completely stressing yourself out, but realize that this is where JiTT gets its name from—the just-in-time processing of student responses for use in the class within the next 10–12 hours. Most course management systems (such as Blackboard or Moodle) allow you to turn off access to JiTT exercises or submissions at a certain time, an easy way of enforcing deadlines. Make sure that students are aware of and understand these deadlines by making announcements in class, posting announcements in the course management system, emailing, or texting students. In most cases, students' JiTT responses are not made public to other students in the course, although some instructors find that making the student responses public is a valuable learning tool.

Analyzing Students' JiTT Responses

Next to developing the JiTT questions, analyzing and organizing students' JiTT responses in preparation for in-class use or follow-up activities is arguably the most important part of the JiTT process. This is your opportunity to really get a good picture of students' thinking processes—while there is time to act on these processes—and use those observations to enhance in-class learning. Once the submission deadline for student responses has passed you have only a few hours before class to make decisions how best to use the responses, so thinking ahead of time about the process of how you will capture, sort, and summarize student responses is important.

Although course management systems vary in how you can view students' JiTT submissions, it is best if you can view all of the submissions sequentially on one screen, or cut-and-paste these submissions into a word processor, where you can then highlight, cut and paste, and rearrange the responses as necessary. As you begin reading JiTT responses you will typically notice that the responses fall into a fairly well-defined set of categories. After having taught the course once, it is generally easy to predict what these will be. However, one of the advantages of using JiTT in your course is that you will sometimes be surprised by the responses that students provide, creating "I never would have known that" or "I never would have thought of that" moments that can be useful for classroom discussion. As you are reading, you might make some notes about different categories of student learning challenges that are appearing so that you can select samples of actual student responses to show in class. In fact, you might want to preliminarily highlight (by bolding, using the digital highlighter, or changing text color) some particularly useful responses as you go along so that they are easy to select later.

After going through all the JiTT responses, select representative examples for class discussion, leaving the students' name off the responses. Even though the responses will be shown anonymously, if possible make sure that all students get to see their responses at some point during the course to maintain motivation for completing the JiTT assignments. After the first time through the course you may be able to quickly identify the half dozen or so responses that will be shown to the class.

Showing student responses in class has a transformational effect on the classroom environment, especially when used at the start of a class session. In our experience, the impact on students' motivation and engagement of seeing their own responses projected in class is quite dramatic, especially if students feel that their responses are being used to shape what occurs in the class period and in the course. The fact that the wording actually comes from students in the class makes the lesson fresh and interesting to the students. In addition to using student responses to the topic-related JiTT questions, note the "what is still unclear" responses and determine whether there are patterns in these responses that need to be addressed in class or whether individual responses are necessary. Again, these comments very often yield valuable pedagogical insight, and explicitly referencing these responses in class generates additional student "buy-in" for the JiTT process.

Finally, after selecting representative responses to present in class, use patterns observed in the full set of responses to revise the lesson flow for the day—whether determining the topics for mini-lectures, in-class personal response quiz questions, demonstrations, or cooperative learning activities. This part of the JiTT pedagogy may seem to be a daunting task, given that the responses are being analyzed just a few hours before class, but experienced faculty members will anticipate student responses and will have activities "ready to go" that address typical student challenges highlighted in the JiTT exercise. Typically, getting ready for class then involves only minor changes in the pre-planned activities, depending on the student responses received. The most important point here is to make the connections between the JiTT exercise, the student responses, and the in-class activity as explicit as possible. Paying attention to this "alignment" among JiTT components will not only reinforce student learning but will also increase students' motivation for completing future JiTT exercises.

Using JiTT in the Classroom

As noted previously, JiTT responses are used in two ways in class: (a) as the source of sample student responses that are directly presented, and (b) to inform and shape classroom activities.

(a) Displaying Student Responses. Using actual student responses in class to present and discuss course content is a fundamental difference between a JiTT class and a traditional lecture or discussion-based class. When students bring their own unique background knowledge to bear in their individual JiTT responses, common misunderstandings often emerge from those responses, misunderstandings that might otherwise remain hidden to both the student and faculty member in courses grounded in more traditional teaching practices. As noted earlier, student responses are typically shown anonymously at the start of class as a jumping-off point for class discussion and activities.

Seeing a selection of student responses, and then using the responses for classroom discussion, is an important tool to sharpen students' learning and communication skills. Students can be asked to defend or refute a particular response, compare and contrast responses, synthesize the ideas in responses to generate a "model" response, etc. The possibilities are endless, reflecting the flexibility of JiTT pedagogy. Table 1.2 provides general recommendations for using JiTT responses in class, along with useful "starting points" for generating student discussion, whether in small groups or as part of a full class discussion. The chapters that follow illustrate how instructors in a variety of disciplines use JiTT responses to promote student learning in their classrooms.

Table 1.2. Using JiTT Responses in Class

General recommendations:
Show some good answers, not just weak ones.
Always treat student responses positively. Never use them to criticize.
Vary the authors of student responses shown in class.
Focus on the thought processes involved in the responses, not the mechanics of the response.
Use questions that are open-ended and promote discussion.
Use student responses as a jumping-off point for in-class discussion and activities.

Questions that promote discussion:
This makes sense, but how could we add to this response? What might be missing?
This is all true, but what if something else occurs simultaneously?
The answer is correct, but how can the reasoning behind the answer be improved?
Compare and contrast the responses that you see.
This has a great beginning, but what else could be added?
This is a great answer, but why isn't this answering the question that was asked?
This is the right idea, but how else might you interpret this response?
What part of this is completely correct? What part is not completely correct?
Under what circumstances would these answers be correct?
What word or two could be changed to fix this completely?
What is particularly good about this response? How could it be improved?

Questions that extend or expand the topic:
What generalizations can we draw from this particular case?
What conditions are specific to this question?
What are the assumptions underlying this question?
Is this true for other cases? Which?
When is this statement false? What happens then?
Is this similar to something we have done before? What?

Questions for using "dueling responses"
Are they exclusive? If so, why? If not, why?
Which response is correct? Why?

(b) Using JiTT Responses to Inform Follow-up In-class Activities. The more that you can integrate JiTT questions and responses into your course, the more effective this teaching and learning strategy will be for both students and instructors. Ideally, students' responses to JiTT questions are used to intentionally inform and shape in-class activities in addition to providing a starting point for class discussions. In many cases, JiTT exercises parallel in-class activities, demonstrations, or experiments that you are already implementing. JiTT exercises help to sharpen the focus of these activities and provide targeted support for learning challenges faced by your students (and revealed in their JiTT responses). For discipline-specific in-class activities see the following chapters in this book.

Assessing JiTT Responses: Grades and Rubrics

In most cases faculty members use JiTT not only as a formative tool to provide insights into student learning, but also include student performance on JiTT exercises as part of course grades. The reasons for doing this are clear: providing extrinsic credit toward a course grade increases student motivation for completing JiTT exercises. The key is making JiTT exercises "count" enough to make it worthwhile for students to genuinely engage in the activity while not undermining the formative foundation of JiTT pedagogy. Typically, making completion of JiTT exercises 5–10% of the total course grade is enough to produce a consistent 80–90% participation rate. Clearly, the extent to which JiTT is integrated into classroom instruction has an impact on this outcome.

Although typically included in course grades, it is important to keep in mind that JiTT assignments are primarily a formative assessment tool aimed at improving learning. JiTT exercises focus on concepts or topics that have not yet been covered formally in class. Students are encouraged to draw on a variety of resources to complete the exercises, but the resulting responses are still likely to exhibit a novice-like understanding of the subject. As a result, credit should be awarded mainly for effort, not for correctness. Experience over a wide range of courses, instructors, settings, and disciplines has shown repeatedly that students will put in the effort to complete JiTT assignments if the work they do is a visible and valued part of the in-class activities. But the question remains: how do I grade on "effort" rather than the "correctness" of the answer?

The simplest solution is to give all students who have submitted a response to the JiTT exercise by the submission deadline "full credit," regardless of quality. However, as many instructors know, this provides an incentive for students to wait until the last minute to get the assignment done, a process that defeats the purpose of thoughtful reflection and reduces the quality of the responses. To increase the quality of responses without creating an undue grading burden, Kathy Marrs, the faculty member highlighted in the opening example in this chapter, has developed a valuable rubric for assessing JiTT responses. The rubric, shown below, is simple enough to be applied quickly and general enough to be used in a wide variety of disciplines. It is particularly helpful for efficiently determining student effort, thoroughness of students' thought processes, student misconceptions, use of available resources, and even how well a particular JiTT question was constructed.

Table 1.3. A Sample JiTT Scoring Rubric

Points	Criteria	Indicators
1	Minimal effort	Student says he/she does not know how to answer the JiTT question.
2	Incorrect answer Low effort	Student tries to answer the JiTT question but does not show evidence of any previous knowledge to assist in answering. Student may reveal misconceptions about concepts. Student does not use any information from the text or lecture notes to answer the question.
3	Partially correct answer but still incomplete Medium effort	Student shows some prior knowledge and may use terminology to answer the JiTT question but does not provide complete explanation for answer. Student does not use appropriate information from the text or lecture notes to answer the question.
4	Correct or nearly correct answer High effort	Student answers the JiTT question with few or no mistakes and provides complete explanation for answer. Student incorporates information from the text or class notes into the answer. Student may look for answer outside the class (Web, etc.).

[Adapted from deCaprariis, Barman, & Magee (2001) by Kathy Marrs]

Note that the scoring is focused on both the level of effort and the correctness of the answer, but that the primary focus is on the effort put forth in trying to answer the questions correctly and completely. With practice and feedback most students should be able to complete JiTT assignments with scores of 3 or 4. To maintain student effort throughout the course it is important to "grade" the JiTT exercises as soon as possible after the submission deadline and provide an up-to-date record of JiTT scores that is easily accessible to students. Most course management systems include a gradebook that simplifies this process.

DOING JiTT: A SUMMARY

The JiTT pedagogy is illustrated in Figure 1.2 below. As outlined above, JiTT is based on a multi-step process intentionally aimed at meeting course learning objectives, focusing out-of-class student learning, informing in-class learning activities, and providing feedback to both instructors and students on the learning process. The process begins with the development of JiTT questions aimed at preparing students for in-class activities, promoting active engagement in the subject matter, and uncovering student difficulties. How students' responses are used to inform the content and activities of the upcoming class period varies by assignment and instructor, but typically involves showing a subset of student responses at the beginning of class, a discussion based on the responses, and a related follow-up in-class activity that gets students actively involved in the JiTT topic.

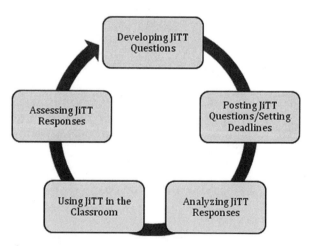

Figure 1.2 The JiTT Process from the Instructor's Perspective

Grounded in research on student learning and effective teaching practices, JiTT pedagogy is adaptable to a wide variety of disciplines, course levels, institution types, and teaching and learning styles, and can be combined with a variety of other pedagogies already being used. What sets JiTT apart from other pedagogical innovations is the intentional focus on using student-generated responses to make the learning process visible and to use those responses to inform in-class activities and discussion. It is the formative aspect of this pedagogy that promotes student engagement in the learning process.

USING JiTT TO MOTIVATE STUDENT LEARNING

Student motivation in many college courses is quite low, especially when the course is a required course outside the student's major. JiTT pedagogy can help improve student motivation by incorporating examples relevant to students' lives in JiTT exercises and asking students to relate course concepts to their own lives. It is not uncommon for instructors to report substantially increased student interest in course-related concepts as a result of integrating JiTT into their courses, especially in science courses like physics and chemistry.

With JiTT assignments due just a few hours before class, instructors try to establish a context for the upcoming lesson content and pique student interest enough to create a need to know. Questions that place students in real-life situations or draw on students' prior experience are particularly effective in building this type of interest. Research shows that students who find the material interesting, useful, and important are more likely to use deeper learning strategies, including metacognitive control (Pintrich, 1989). In addition, research findings suggest that more meaningful learning occurs when course content is integrated with students' prior knowledge (Anderson, 1990). Good JiTT questions challenge students to integrate new course content and ideas with their existing knowledge, including previous life experiences. This process works best when the JiTT exercise produces "desirable difficulties" for students without overwhelming them.

JiTT REQUIRES CHANGES FOR BOTH STUDENTS AND TEACHERS

Redefining Learning (and the Role of the Learner)

JiTT is very different for most students, who are not in the habit of having their work regularly influence what occurs in the classroom. Nor are students used to seeing their work used as the basis for class discussion. As a result, instructors need to prepare students for JiTT, both in terms of its structure and its purpose. When students are first exposed to JiTT they often find it challenging to manage their time and work in small, daily installments. Hence, it is important to have clear deadlines for submission and easy-to-understand policies for grading.

Another area of student preparation involves the formative nature of JiTT exercises and follow-up in-class activities. In most classes, students are used to getting the "right answer." With JiTT, there may not be a "right" answer, although some JiTT responses are better than others, as evidenced by the rubric illustrated in Table 1.3. Because JiTT assignments are designed to expose deficiencies in prior knowledge and to elicit fallacies in preconceptions, student responses are often incomplete, at least from the perspective of an "expert." To promote learning, it is important that students don't see "wrong" answers as evidence of failure. JiTT exercises are done at the start of the learning process for a given topic or concept, so incomplete knowledge is to be expected. Rather, what is expected of students and rewarded is evidence of effortful thinking and thoughtful reflection on the thinking process. Each discipline will experience its own version of this issue, yet the underlying premise is consistent across JiTT applications. To be effective, students are asked to examine and evaluate their own points of view and the points of view of other students. It is important that instructors share with students why this leads to deeper and more permanent learning.[2]

Redefining Teaching (and the Role of the Teacher)

The transition from traditional, teacher-centered instruction to an instructional strategy that puts active student engagement squarely in the middle of the teaching and learning process requires time, reflection, and practice. For most of us this is not how we were taught. However, once the decision to change teaching and learning practices is made, one has to proceed slowly and deliberately, allowing the students to provide feedback along the way. In addition, it might prove helpful to a prospective adopter of a new teaching practice to do some background reading on transitions in professional practices.

Particularly useful is the reflective practitioner model developed by Donald Schön in the 1980s (Schön; 1983, 1987). As described in Wilson & Cole (1992), Schön suggests a developmental sequence that typically characterizes the change process associated with the adoption of new pedagogical methods by instructors: (1) routinized responses to situations (e.g. continuing with past teaching methods), (2) an unexpected outcome that draws our attention (e.g. concerns about high failure rates in a course), (3) reflection about the unexpected outcome and recasting of the "problem" (e.g. considering

Table 1.4. Tips for Teaching Success with JiTT

Allow for trial and error in developing JiTT materials.

Be sensitive to students' ideas, attitudes, and state of knowledge.

Constantly monitor the progress of students' learning.

Have a firm understanding of the material to appreciate and respond to students' ideas.

Be creative and develop learning tasks that support this kind of learning.

Maintain a classroom climate where everybody is free to participate within a structured environment.

---

alternate ways of addressing the unexpected outcome), and (4) trying out a new perspective and noting its affects (e.g. adopting a new teaching strategy). JiTT provides one avenue for addressing unexpected student learning outcomes such as high failure rates, but its success requires instructors to recreate their view of the role of students in that process, as well as their own role as teachers. In particular, instructors who adapt JiTT pedagogy for their own courses need to continually keep in mind the formative nature of JiTT, its ability to uncover student misunderstandings, and its value in informing classroom teaching and learning. JiTT puts students at the middle of the teaching and learning process, a process that requires faculty members to substitute student feedback for classroom authority. The art of using JiTT involves the use of this feedback to create a learning environment that fosters student engagement, responds to student learning challenges, and develops critical and reflective learners.

Table 1.4 provides a list of useful tips to make your transition to the JiTT method as smooth as possible. The best advice is to start off with only a few JiTT exercises in your classes and increase the frequency of these exercises over time. As you get comfortable with the JiTT strategy and the process of analyzing students' JiTT responses you will find more and more ways to integrate JiTT pedagogy into your courses. Use the ideas presented in the remaining chapters in this book to spur your own creative ideas on how to make JiTT work for you and your students.

JiTT RESOURCES

JiTT practitioners can share their materials and experiences by visiting the JiTT digital library at www.jittdl.org. Developed with a grant from the National Science Foundation National Science Digital Library (NSDL) program, the library consists of a collections site, a wiki, and a hosting site for first-time users who may not have access to a university-level course management system.[3] The collections site contains sample JiTT material from pioneering developers in biology, chemistry, earth science, economics, mathematics, physics, and psychology. The annotated entries contain a variety of JiTT exercises, many with student responses. These exercises can be used directly in your classes or can be adapted to suit the particular course or topic that you are teaching. Again, the flexibility of JiTT is one of its great strengths. We expect the collection to grow with continuing contributions from new and seasoned practitioners.

The hosting site included as part of the JiTT digital library allows first-time users to post JiTT assignments and retrieve student responses online without having to maintain their own course management system. The responses can be scored online and can also be viewed by instructors in many JiTT-friendly formats. Further, the responses can be sorted by student names, by question number, and in other ways. The wiki is intended to serve as a virtual faculty lounge and discussion board. Registered users can annotate one another's reflections on a variety of issues, including lesson development, classroom implementation, and assessment. We encourage you to join this community of JiTT users and developers by registering at the digital library site.[4] In the meantime, we hope that you will take full advantage of the ideas presented in this book to begin experimenting with JiTT in your own classes.

Notes

1. National Science Foundation DUE 9752365. During the last decade additional support for the JiTT effort has been provided by the National Science Foundation, Prentice-Hall Publishing Company, the American Association of Physics Teachers (AAPT), the Digital Library for Earth System Education (DLESE), and Project Kaleidoscope.

2. For more on this issue see Scott, Asoko, & Driver (1991, p.10)

3. Eric Mazur and Jessica Watkins (chapter 3, this volume) also provide links to a freely-available tool for posting JiTT questions and submitting/reviewing JiTT responses online.

4. In addition, the Science Education Resource Center (SERC) at Carleton College (MN) provides a pedagogic portal, *Pedagogy in Action* <http://serc.carleton.edu/sp/index.html>, featuring JiTT <http://serc.carleton.edu/sp/library/justintime/index.html> and many other innovative teaching pedagogies. The site includes a description of JiTT, JiTT research, how to use JiTT, and a library of JiTT examples.

References

Anderson, J. (1990). *Cognitive psychology and its implications.* New York: Freeman

Bransford, J. D., Brown, A. L., & Cocking, R. R. (Eds.). (2000). *How people learn: Brain, mind, experience, and school.* Washington, DC: National Academy Press.

deCaprariis, P., Barman, C., & Magee, P. (2001). Monitoring the benefits of active learning exercises in introductory survey courses in science: An attempt to improve the education of prospective public school teachers. *The Journal of Scholarship of Teaching and Learning, 1*(2), 1–11.

Novak, G. M., Patterson, E. T., Gavrin, A. D., & Christian, W. (1999). *Just-in-time teaching: Blending active learning with web technology.* Upper Saddle River, NJ: Prentice Hall.

Pintrich, P. R. (1989). The dynamic interplay of student motivation and cognition in the college classroom. In C. Ames & M. Maehr (Eds.), *Advances in motivation and achievement: Motivation-enhancing environments (Vol. 6)* (pp. 117–160). Greenwich: JAI Press.

Schön, D. (1983). *The reflective practitioner.* New York: Basic Books.

Schön, D. (1987). *Educating the reflective practitioner: Toward a new design for teaching and learning in the professions.* San Francisco: Jossey-Bass.

Scott, P. H., Asoko, H. M., & Driver, R. H. (1991). Teaching for conceptual change: A review of strategies. In R. Duit, F. Goldberg, & H. Neidderer (Eds.), *Research in physics learning: Theoretical issues and empirical studies,* (pp. 310–329). Keil, Germany: Schmidt & Klannig.

Wilson, B., & Cole, P. (1992). A critical review of elaboration theory. *Educational Technology Research and Development, 40*(3), 63–79

2

Using Just-in-Time Teaching to Motivate Student Learning

Mary Elizabeth Camp, Joan Middendorf,
and Carol Subiño Sullivan

This chapter[1] examines the challenge of using Just-in-Time Teaching (JiTT) to motivate student learning. Based on studies of JiTT pedagogy over two semesters in a large Indiana University statistics course, we found that *how* JiTT is implemented matters a great deal in terms of its impact on student motivation and learning. During the first semester of JiTT implementation, peer researchers directly observed students as they completed JiTT exercises prior to class, and a follow-up survey asked students about their practices and attitudes regarding JiTT exercises. The results indicated that many students put in minimal effort on the exercises or ignored them altogether, a finding confirmed by feedback from students in the course.

Based on student feedback, we greatly modified our implementation of JiTT in the second semester, explaining to students more carefully (and frequently) the role of JiTT exercises in promoting learning in the course and rewriting JiTT exercises to encourage deeper thinking about course concepts and increase students' reflection on their own learning processes. The result was greater student participation in JiTT exercises, improved formative assessment of student learning gaps, and increased recognition of the value of JiTT exercises as a learning tool.

We believe that the insights gained from our study of JiTT pedagogy and practice, though focused on a particular course and discipline, are general enough to provide valuable information for other instructors who are considering adopting JiTT pedagogy in their own classes, regardless of discipline. In the remainder of this chapter we first describe the framework for our study and the results of the initial implementation of JiTT pedagogy, followed by a discussion of the process we used to make modifications to the JiTT strategy in the next semester. We conclude by summarizing the lessons we learned from our two-semester JiTT design, implementation, assessment, and revision process.

A HARD-EARNED LESSON ABOUT JiTT
AND STUDENT STUDY HABITS

Just-in-Time Teaching has the potential to help students develop study skills that will serve them throughout their learning careers. At the heart of the JiTT process is a set of conceptual questions that students answer electronically prior to class. The resulting responses typically reveal student misconceptions, misunderstandings, and conceptual errors related to the material to be covered in the upcoming lesson. Instructors analyze the student responses before class, using the identified learning gaps to adjust planned classroom instruction "just in time." Further details about the JiTT process are provided in Novak, Patterson, Gavrin, and Christian (1999) and in chapter 1 of this book.

One of the key results of our research is the finding that the JiTT process of assigning frequent, short, conceptual exercises between classes has the potential to modify students' usual study pattern of cramming before exams. However, we have also found that students who resist the JiTT process and continue to cram their studying into brief bursts of intense focus just before exams rather than engaging in regular, moderate study sessions experienced strong negative emotions about JiTT that further interfered with their learning. With these findings in mind, instructors who use JiTT exercises in their courses need to help students understand the structure and benefits of the JiTT process so they will adopt a different time management strategy for their academic work. Without this guidance at the start of a course, students are likely to fall back on old study habits that have worked for them in the past, diluting the benefits of JiTT and potentially creating a negative, rather than positive, JiTT feedback loop.

One of the benefits of using JiTT in a well-understood and structured manner is that it helps students develop more effective study skills that can easily be transferred to other courses. Although this lesson was hard earned for us—students were not learning as much as we hoped with JiTT in the first semester of the study and student attitudes about JiTT were quite negative—we were able to uncover a problem that previously had gone unnoticed. By finding out what our students actually *did* when they prepared for our course, we were able to redesign JiTT exercises to make them more effective. We believe that other instructors who adopt the JiTT pedagogy can benefit from our experience and avoid the kinds of issues we experienced. JiTT is a valuable tool for improving student learning, but *how* it is implemented matters a great deal in ensuring its success.

STUDY BACKGROUND AND THE INITIAL USE OF JiTT EXERCISES

To see how students actually complete JiTT exercises, we observed students enrolled in a large (over 300 students) introductory statistics course intended for business/economics majors and taught in a large lecture/small lab environment. The course goal was to enable students to perform data analysis using statistical tools and data encountered in future classes or on the job. JiTT exercises played an integral role in the design of this course, with the aim of focusing students' out-of-class study time on key course topics—prior to formal in-class instruction. In the first semester of this study JiTT exercises consisted of three multiple-choice questions posted online in the course management system. This format facilitated the analysis of hundreds of responses in a timely fashion prior to the lecture. Students were allowed to access the exercises one time during the twenty-four hour period immediately prior to class and had a limit of 20 minutes to complete and submit their responses.[2] JiTT exercises accounted for 5% of students' final grades and students could miss one of the three questions on each JiTT exercise and still obtain full credit.

An example of an actual JiTT exercise used about three weeks into the course is shown below. This question was aimed at uncovering student confusion regarding two related statistical measures.

The Interquartile Range is designed to overcome the failings of the Range due to the Range's:
   a. sensitivity to outliers.
   b. use of limited information.
   c. inability to describe how data points are grouped within the data set.
   d. simplicity of calculation.

The question was answered correctly ("a" is the correct answer) by 86% of the students, signaling to the instructor that little time needed to be spent on this item in class.

In another JiTT exercise, the following question was used to explore students' ability to distinguish between the concepts of correlation and causality, a common source of confusion for students in statistics courses.

Based on 1988 census data for the 50 states in the United States, the correlation between the number of churches per state and the number of violent crimes per state was 0.85. We can conclude that:
   a. the relationship is not causal because only correlations of +1 or −1 show causal relationships.

b. there is a causal relationship between the number of churches and the number of violent crimes committed in a city.

c. the correlation is spurious because both the number of churches and the number of violent crimes are related to the population size.

d. because the data comes from a census, or nearly complete enumeration of the United States, there must be a causal relationship between the number of churches and the number of violent crimes.

In this case only 59% of the students selected the correct answer (c), while 29% of the students incorrectly selected (b). On the basis of this feedback, the instructor used the lecture time in the following class to focus on the differences between causality and correlation. A unit defining causation was included, followed by an in-class activity that required student teams to determine whether a causal relationship existed between specified variable pairs and why.

In addition to uncovering learning gaps such as the one illustrated in the example above, one of the most useful aspects of JiTT is that it signals to students that the instructor is interested in finding out whether they truly understand important course concepts prior to class and is willing to structure upcoming class activities to directly address learning challenges identified by the JiTT exercise responses.

DIGGING DEEPER INTO JiTT: WHAT DO STUDENTS ACTUALLY DO WHEN COMPLETING JiTT EXERCISES?

In this study we wanted to find out how students actually complete JiTT exercises outside of class. According to Tomanek & Montplaisir (2004, p. 254), "... (p)ostsecondary learning environments generally are built on the assumption that students are responsible for their own learning opportunities," raising the initial question for our research, "What do students actually do when they study?"

Data collection was designed and completed in collaboration with a team of undergraduate researchers who had successfully completed the course during the previous term. Using undergraduates as research assistants provided us with a rich picture of the thought processes and practices students engaged in when completing their JiTT exercises. We found that students were more willing to share their honest responses with fellow students than with older researchers. The student researchers were trained in ethnographic interview and observation methods, including Human Subjects Procedures, during several practice sessions in which they interviewed each other or friends working on homework assignments or problems. The research team then discussed the practice interviews so that successful strategies could be identified and the process refined. Finally, we set up a time and space where the student researchers could interact with the statistics students while the latter worked on actual JiTT exercises.

The researchers asked simple questions that prompted the students to explain their decision-making process out loud with such questions as: "What are you going to try first?"; "Why did you consult that resource?" and "How did you find that answer?"[3] The researcher recorded all of the student's responses in a notebook as well as making note of observations about the student's behaviors. During the data collection sessions one of the authors monitored the lab environment and made sure all participants were properly checked in and informed about the study's purpose.[4] To follow up on our observations, we developed a web-based survey that asked students further questions about their practices and attitudes regarding JiTT exercises.

WHAT DID WE FIND?

During two lab sessions we invited students to complete their JiTT exercises while our research team observed and asked questions about their thought processes. Most students flipped through the course text, workbook or lab manual in order to search for clues to the answers *after* they had already opened the assignment and the 20-minute timer was ticking. This observed behavior was supported by responses to our survey in which 80% of students reported spending almost no time preparing for JiTT exercises before attempting to complete them. Such a strategy is likely to fail because JiTT exercises often require students to connect both previous and new material and articulate what is confusing or challenging about the concept under consideration.

Many students tried to get around this problem by sharing answers to the JiTT questions. At our sessions many students had already been advised of the answers from a friend (perhaps even been told while they were waiting in line to enter the lab!) and either simply entered the answers or did some minimal flipping through resources to confirm that the answers were correct. With only 33% of students reporting that they took advantage of the JiTT exercises to help them learn, the majority of students who came to these sessions were not putting deep thought or effort into the exercises and thus not gaining from them what they could.

Studying for JiTT exercises presented a serious challenge for our students: they would have to apply themselves in order to answer the questions correctly, a problem of process and work habit rather than technique. In their responses to our survey, students named a number of study strategies they could call upon to learn and review difficult material: reading, making note cards, working in peer groups, asking the instructor questions, solving practice problems, seeking tutoring, doing online research, focusing more, spending some time doing the assignments each day, and visiting office hours. Despite student awareness of these good study habits, students' study instincts were apparently not triggered by JiTT exercises, at least in our laboratory sessions.

Additionally, students had a distorted understanding of the type of effort expected for JiTT exercises. In our survey, students indicated that they needed to study for only a few hours, or at most a few days, in advance of exams or other graded assessments in the course to do well. Because cramming had worked for most students in the past, they did not trust that regular, moderate study sessions would actually help them to approach the material any better. As a result, they continued to follow their previous study habits when completing JiTT exercises. Predictably, this behavior meant that students had difficulty sorting out what they did and did not know in these exercises. Although these students were masterful at rallying in the face of intense challenges and making a strong finish in cramming for exams, they did not understand how to manage their study time deliberately in smaller chunks over the long term when it came to JiTT exercises.

Unfortunately for students who follow the last-minute approach, JiTT can lead to negative results. For example, some students fell behind as they failed to complete the JiTT exercises and thus missed the rehearsal of concepts prior to class that would have helped them integrate new and previously introduced material. By the time we collected data a few weeks before the end of the semester, they realized that they might miss out completely on the JiTT points and now were at risk of failing. No amount of cramming would give them back the points nor the practice they had lost by not steadily applying themselves all along. It was at this point near the end of the semester that we collected data, so it is no wonder that the students, feeling resentful, lashed out in their responses to our survey questions.

REVISING OUR STRATEGY

Caught off guard by the unexpectedly high levels of negative affect we found in our analysis of the students' surveys and interviews, we turned to the literature on emotions and learning. How could we better understand and deal with student resistance to JiTT so that students would be more likely to thoughtfully complete JiTT exercises throughout the course? Our research led us to useful insights about student compliance with reading assignments and the role that emotions play in the learning process, information that we used to revise the structure of JiTT exercises to boost student motivation and engagement with respect to the JiTT exercises.

According to self-reported data from the first semester of the study, only 33% of students took advantage of the JiTT exercises to help them learn, a result that is consistent with the research on compliance with course readings. According to Hobson (2004), such studies have repeatedly found that only 20–30% of students complete any given reading assignment. To increase JiTT participation in the second semester of the project, we:

1. provided more frequent explanations of the JiTT exercises, including their impact on improving student learning.
2. explained more carefully what students could expect to gain from completing JiTT exercises, and
3. offered guidance about where students could get the necessary information to answer the JiTT exercise.

In addition, we followed Hobson's recommendation that short writing assignments be used to increase compliance with reading assignments—we moved to open-ended JiTT questions. Our hope was that switching from a multiple choice to a short-answer format would motivate students to take advantage of JiTT exercises to practice their understanding of course concepts and ideas. Interestingly, we found that when given the chance in the second semester to reflect on what they found most interesting or difficult about the readings for each lesson, 97% of students produced detailed replies, a much higher rate of compliance than in the previous semester.

In addition to increasing participation in reading assignments, open-ended questions provide a mechanism for asking more authentic, data-based questions that require students to reason statistically and explain their thought processes in writing. On a pedagogical level, open-ended questions provide the opportunity to ask students to practice thinking deeply about statistical concepts. As Garfield (2002) notes, "making interpretations based on sets of data, graphical representations, and statistical summaries" exemplifies what is meant by statistical reasoning, a core goal of statistics courses. Using open-ended JiTT questions provided many more opportunities for students to practice these key learning activities.

In addition to changing the format of JiTT questions, we also addressed the emotional aspects of learning. Beard, Clegg, & Smith (2007), Zembylas (2007), and Nuhfer (2005) argue that educational research has focused to a great extent on the cognitive aspects of learning, with the affective aspects less well understood. Svinicki (2005) provides pragmatic advice for managing the affective dimension of student learning by providing five key recommendations for reducing the risk of failure:

1. Show interest in and support for mistakes.
2. Provide opportunities for students to make multiple attempts without severe penalties.
3. Model how to learn from and correct mistakes.
4. Offer credit for making progress.
5. Create a community where everyone helps each other learn, rather than being perfect.

We used Svinicki's recommendations as a framework to rethink the structure of the JiTT exercises to improve student motivation and engagement in the JiTT process.

Show interest in and support for mistakes. A key function of JiTT exercises is to uncover errors in student thinking processes and address them. Both the multiple choice and open-ended JiTT question formats can be effective in meeting this goal. Svinicki's principle reminded us of the necessity of telling students up front and at regular intervals why they are doing JiTT exercises and how we can learn from mistakes. Specific errors are presented, analyzed, and corrected using additional in-class exercises, mini-lectures, and assessments. The multiple choice format makes it easy to analyze which items students had difficulty with for use in the JiTT lecture. Analysis of the open-ended responses was not as clear. Although it was relatively easy to estimate the proportion of students who had trouble with a question, it was difficult to sort out what concept(s) in the question gave the students trouble.

Provide opportunities for students to make multiple attempts without severe penalties. Our first semester revealed that students routinely "shared" answers to multiple choice JiTT questions, even though the policy of allowing only a single attempt had been expressly applied in an effort to thwart this behavior. To motivate student participation in the second semester, learners were given two days to answer open-ended questions. The new response policy also allowed as many attempts as the student desired (although only about 1 percent completed more than one attempt.). Together, these two changes helped to reduce time pressures associated with JiTT exercises. Graders during the second semester of the study indicated that they saw no more than one copied response per activity, on average. In addition, on average 97% of the students submitted JiTT responses on a given assignment over the course of the semester, a dramatically high response rate.

Model how to learn from and correct mistakes. During the second semester of the study we added two additional questions to each JiTT exercise: "What single concept or idea did you find most confusing or most difficult in the readings for this lesson? If nothing was confusing or difficult, what did you find of most interest?" This pair of questions fostered meta-cognitive reflection, providing students the time and space to reflect on how they were doing individually and where they were having problems. Graders summarized the responses to this question, which proved invaluable to the professor. While summaries often reflected the areas of confusion already revealed in the content-related questions, unexpected problems were sometimes exposed.

It might seem reasonable to simply use this question by itself, in place of the three content-specific questions, in order to cut down on the amount of time needed to review and grade the responses. However, the results achieved would not be as informative. Forcing students to wrestle with and respond to the three specific content-related questions helps students to discover areas of confusion. Many students took great pains to write complete responses to the questions. As a result, the responses contained a wealth of material for assessing and improving the quality of the JiTT questions prior to future use.

Offer credit for making progress. By relying on multiple choice JiTT questions during the first semester, students were explicitly rewarded for "getting the right answer." During the second semester of the study, students were reminded at the start of each JiTT exercise that: "Each response will be scored based on three criteria: you will receive credit for this exercise if your answer is thoughtful, serious, and original." Although penalties were possible, they resulted only from non-responses, plagiarized answers, and frivolous or gibberish responses. Students received points for making reasonable attempts to respond to the questions.

Create a community where everyone helps each other learn, rather than being perfect. Students were placed in permanent teams that worked on exercises and problems together in class and in the statistics lab, with team participation encouraged and rewarded both semesters. However, the open-ended JiTT format, coupled with a longer submission period, fostered a focus on learning, rather than being perfect. As a consequence, the learning teams worked more communally in the second semester than in the first semester.

Overall, by changing the format and the submission period of the JiTT exercises, we were able to incorporate all five of Svinicki's recommendations, providing greater motivation for student participation in the JiTT process, both in and out of class.

EXAMPLES OF THE NEW FORMAT

Here is an example of a JiTT question using the new, open-ended response format adopted in the second semester.

What does a statistician mean when speaking of the "dispersion" of a data set? How does the "range" measure dispersion?

Two representative student responses to this question are shown below:

Student 1:

Dispersions are measures that help us make judgments about how similar observations in a data set are to each other. The range is the simplest to calculate, and it measures how far apart the highest value from the lowest value in the set are.

Student 2:

The meaning of dispersion when talking about statistics is the spread of the data set. Which means the distance between numbers in the data set [sic]. The range measures dispersion by measuring the difference from the smallest set to the largest set. This allows statisticians to have a better understanding of the size of the data set.

The value of the open-ended responses in providing useful formative assessment of student learning is immediately obvious. The first response succinctly responds to the question and shows evidence of a clear understanding of this topic. The second response, however, illustrates at least two areas of confusion: (1) the student is demonstrating a misunderstanding of the difference between a value in a data set and the data set itself and (2) the student is equating dispersion with the size of a sample. This type of feedback can be used to target in-class instruction to specific issues revealed in the students' JiTT responses. Although responses to multiple-choice questions let the instructor know whether students are "getting" the material, they don't provide insights into *why* they are having trouble with the material. Open-ended questions provide much richer information about the sources of students' learning gaps.

In this case, based on the JiTT responses, the instructor had a clear idea of which topics to include in the upcoming class and the types of activities to develop for the in-class teamwork exercises. The class began with a mini-lecture reinforcing the meaning of the term "range" in statistics and comparing and contrasting this measure of dispersion with other measures introduced previously in the course. In addition, definitions of related statistical terms were reviewed.

For the in-class team-based activity, artificial data sets were presented with varying ranges and sample sizes. Student teams were presented with a set of ranges from different variables and asked to describe what they knew about each variable based on its range. Student teams quickly worked through the activity and team reports indicated that most student teams now had little difficulty with the concepts being presented. Because the activity had taken little time, students were presented with a multiple choice assessment question in which a specific variable was described and its range reported. Classroom response technology indicated few students continued to have difficulty with the concept.

In every JiTT exercise, the reflective question "What did you find most confusing, difficult or interesting?" is asked, yielding responses such as the following:

- I found the Albert Einstein quote relating to statistics interesting.
- I think this lesson really helped me grasp the idea of a p-value. In the beginning the p-value confused me the most about hypothesis testing. Also, the lab session really helped it all make sense to me. I find it most interesting that there is actually a way to mathematically prove whether or not a hypothesis should be rejected. I find it amazing that people are so smart to come up with this stuff!
- I have no idea how to even begin the second question.
- I'm having trouble understanding how covariance fits into linear equations. Could you do a problem like this in class?
- The lesson explained p-value clearly, but determining H0 and H1 still confuses me.

Without the inclusion of a reflective question as part of the JiTT exercise, these responses would have remained hidden to the instructor. Instead, this information could be incorporated in real time into the upcoming class, efficiently addressing students' concerns. Including this type of reflective question as a part of JiTT exercises allows students to express their emotional reactions to the homework material. When students see this information influencing classroom instruction their motivation for completing future JiTT exercises increases, creating a positive feedback loop.

WHAT WE LEARNED

Our research yielded important insights into the affective nature of student responses and the role that they play in promoting the success or failure of pedagogical innovations. We found that it is important to explain to students how Just-in-Time Teaching works and how it can improve their learning— and grades—in the course. From the beginning of the semester and through-out the course, instructors need to explain carefully to students why JiTT is different than the traditional teaching practices they experience in most of their other courses and how they can adjust their study strategies to get the most benefit from JiTT exercises.

Svinicki's recommendations for managing affect and failure risk pro-vided a valuable framework for redesigning JiTT exercises to better support and improve student motivation. Foremost, we helped students understand the positive role making errors plays in the JiTT process, both by grading JiTT responses on the basis of effort and using students' responses to guide classroom instruction. And despite our ongoing concern about "response-sharing," we implemented Svinicki's second recommendation to allow stu-dents multiple attempts without severe penalty. Not only was little response-sharing perceived, but response rates also suggested an exception-ally high rate of student compliance with assignments. Of course, using open-ended rather than multiple-choice questions also helped to reduce the opportunities for students to simply copy from each other or pass along answers. Instances of answer-sharing are much easier to detect when open-ended JiTT questions are used.

Asking students to reflect on the specific topics or concepts that were most difficult for them emphasized the third recommendation—learning from and correcting mistakes—and required students to participate in metacognitive reflection (a learning practice emphasized in Bransford, Brown, and Cocking's (2000) review of recent learning sciences research). Offering credit for making progress, Svinicki's fourth recommendation, was implemented by eliminating "right" answers, and instead crediting genuine student effort, effectively changing the focus of student perception of the activities from that of a "test" to one of a "learning exercise." The very long time horizon for response submission supported the sense of a "learning com-munity" in the class, reflective of Svinicki's last recommendation.

The results from the first semester of our study revealed that students had a distorted impression about the amount of effort expected to complete JiTT exercises and the role that JiTT exercises were intended to play in the course. Students who were accustomed to cramming as a study strategy resorted to cheating when they had not prepared themselves for the JiTT exercises through regular, moderate study. Only 33% took advantage of JiTT exercises and found them useful. As they fell behind from their lack of effort on these exercises, many students became resentful. In the second semester of the study, after modifying the JiTT strategy based on Svinicki's principles to reduce the risk of failure, very little cheating was observed and very high levels of JiTT completion were maintained throughout the semester. Most importantly, student responses were detailed, thoughtful, and reflective.

SUMMARY

Overall, we have found the integration of JiTT pedagogy into an introductory statistics course to be beneficial for student learning, despite the challenges faced in the first semester of its implementation. Changes we made in the structure of the JiTT questions, how they were introduced to students, and the process of responding to these questions in the second semester of its implementation—all drawn from Svinicki's research on student motivation—made a significant difference in how JiTT was perceived by students. Moreover, the open-ended JiTT responses resulting from the new JiTT framework provided a wealth of information on students' learning and thought processes that otherwise would have remained hidden.

Instructors can use this type of information to inform their in-class teaching activities, allowing them to efficiently target identified student learning gaps. As a result, students feel like their professors care about their learning—and by extension, them—creating a positive feedback loop between the out-of-class JiTT exercises and in-class teaching and learning activities. Indeed, this positive interdependence is the hallmark of the JiTT approach, as illustrated in every chapter in this book. The key lesson to be drawn from our work is that JiTT can be an effective tool for improving student learning in a wide variety of disciplines but its implementation must be accompanied by effective communication with students about its purpose, process, and impact to ensure that its learning potential is fully realized.

Notes

1. An earlier version of this chapter appeared in *National Teaching and Learning Forum*, "Engrained Study Habits and the Challenge of Warmups in Just-in-Time Teaching" (Vol. 17, No. 4, May 2008) by Carol Subiño Sullivan, Joan Middendorf, and Mary Elizabeth Camp, Indiana University.

2. The 20-minute limit was automatically enforced by the course management system and began when students opened the JiTT exercise. After 20 minutes (with appropriate time limit warnings) the course management system would no longer accept students' submissions.

3. This type of procedure is generally referred to as a "think-aloud-protocol" and has been used for decades in both industry and higher education to better understand the actual thought processes underlying the completion of specific tasks, in this case completing JiTT exercises. Physicist education researchers such as Lillian McDermott and E.F. Redish (and their colleagues at the University of Washington and University of Maryland physics education research groups, respectively) have used this technique to uncover and address a wide variety of learning gaps in physics education. See http://www.physics.umd.edu/perg/abp/think/index.html and http://www.phys.washington.edu/groups/peg/ for additional resources and research findings related to this technique.

4. The study was approved by the Indiana University Institutional Review Board and informed consent forms were provided to the students involved in the study.

References

Beard, C., Clegg, S., & Smith, K. (2007). Acknowledging the affective in higher education. *British Educational Research Journal, 33*(2), 235–252.

Bransford, J. D., Brown, A. L., & Cocking, Rodney R. (Eds.). (2000). *How people learn: Brain, mind, experience, and school.* Washington, DC: National Academy Press.

Garfield, J. (2002). The challenge of developing statistical reasoning. *Journal of Statistics Education, 10*(3). Retrieved from http://www.amstat.org/publications/jse/v10n3/garfield.html

Hobson, E. (2004). Getting students to read: Fourteen tips. *IDEA Paper #40.* Retrieved from http://www.theideacenter.org/sites/default/files/Idea_Paper_40.pdf.

Novak, G. M., Patterson, E. T., Gavrin, A. D., & Christian, W. (1999). *Just-in-time teaching: Blending active learning with web technology.* Upper Saddle River, NJ: Prentice Hall.

Nuhfer, E. B. (2005). De Bono's red hat on Krathwohl's head: Irrational means to rational ends. *The National Teaching and Learning Forum, 14*(5) 7–11.

Svinicki, M. (2005). Student goal orientation, motivation, and learning. *IDEA Paper #41.* Retrieved from http://www.idea.ksu.edu/papers/Idea_Paper_41.pdf

Tomanek, D., & Montplaisir, L. (2004). Students' studying and approaches to learning in introductory biology. *Cell Biology Education, 3*(4), 253–262.

Zembylas, M. (2007). Emotional ecology: The intersection of emotional knowledge and pedagogical content knowledge in teaching. *Teaching and Teacher Education, 23*(4), 355–367.

3

Just-in-Time Teaching and Peer Instruction

Jessica Watkins and Eric Mazur

Peer Instruction (PI) is an interactive teaching technique that promotes classroom interaction to engage students and address difficult aspects of the material (Crouch, Watkins, Fagen, & Mazur, 2007; Crouch & Mazur, 2001; Mazur, 1997). By providing opportunities for students to discuss concepts in class, PI allows students to learn from each other. However, for this method to be most effective, students need to come to class with some basic understanding of the material. Just-in-Time Teaching (JiTT) is an ideal complement to PI, as JiTT structures students' reading before class and provides feedback so the instructor can tailor the PI questions to target student difficulties.

Separately, both JiTT and PI provide students with valuable feedback on their learning at different times in the process—JiTT works asynchronously out of class, and PI gives real-time feedback. Together, these methods help students and instructors monitor learning as it happens, strengthening the benefits of this feedback. As this chapter details, the combination of these methods is useful for improving student learning and skill development.

PEER INSTRUCTION AND JUST-IN-TIME TEACHING: THE BASICS

How PI Works. This book includes many descriptions of how JiTT can help successfully prepare students by structuring reading before class. In comparison, PI structures time during class around short, conceptual multiple-choice questions, known as ConcepTests, an example of which is shown in Figure 3.1. These questions are targeted to address student difficulties and promote student thinking about challenging concepts.

The ConcepTest procedure is depicted in Figure 3.2. After a brief presentation by the instructor, the focus shifts from the instructor to the student, as the instructor encourages the students to think about the material by posing a ConcepTest.

A blood platelet drifts along with the flow of blood through an artery that is partially blocked by deposits.

As the platelet moves from the narrow region to the wider region, its speed

1. increases.
2. remains the same.
3. decreases.

Figure 3.1. A Sample ConcepTest

After 1–2 minutes of thinking, students commit to an individual answer. If an appropriate percentage of students answer the ConcepTest correctly, the instructor asks students to turn to their neighbors and discuss their answers. Students talk in pairs or small groups and are encouraged to find someone with a different answer. The teaching staff circulates throughout the room to encourage productive discussions and guide student thinking. After several minutes students answer the same ConcepTest again. The instructor then explains the correct answer and, depending on the student answers, may pose another related ConcepTest or move on to a different topic.

In science courses PI has been shown to be a useful way to engage students in classroom demonstrations, much like interactive lecture demonstra-

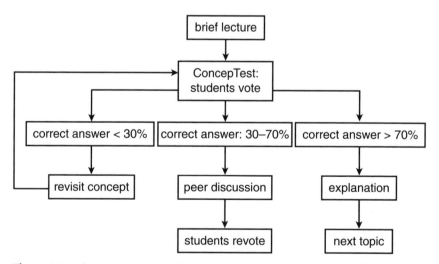

Figure 3.2. The ConcepTest-Peer Instruction Implementation Process. From Lasry et al. (2008). Reprinted with permission. © American Association of Physics Teachers.

tions (Sokoloff and Thornton, 1997). Before showing students what happens when you mix two chemicals or flip a switch on a given circuit, instructors can ask students to predict the outcomes. Research shows that asking students to predict the outcome of an experiment results in greater conceptual understanding (Crouch, Fagen, Callan, & Mazur, 2004) and instructors report increased student engagement (Mazur, 1997). In social science or humanities courses PI can be used to involve the students as participants in experiments with human responses (Draper, Cargill, & Cutts, 2002).

A variety of question-types can be used with PI, including questions about general theories and definitions, questions asking students to apply concepts in different contexts, and questions that illustrate how different ideas are related. PI is not only useful for questions with "correct" answers, but also for promoting discussion among students with questions that lack a clear-cut answer. For example, a ConcepTest may ask students to consider the relative importance of different assumptions in a scientific hypothesis or the relative value of different interpretations of a literary passage. The structure of PI provides opportunities for students to hone their skills in critical listening and developing solid arguments. Regardless of subject matter, PI enables students to create knowledge through discussion and become active participants in the discipline they are studying.

PI and JiTT. The quality of student discussion and learning in a PI classroom depends on the quality of the ConcepTests. Several databases of class-tested questions exist in physics (Mazur, 1997), chemistry (Ellis et al., 2000; Landis et al. 2001), astronomy (Green, 2002), mathematics (Hughes-Hallett et al., 2005; Terrell, 2005), geoscience (Starting Point—Teaching Entry Level Geoscience: ConcepTest Examples, 2008), philosophy (Bigelow, Butchart, & Handfield, 2007), and psychology (Canadian In-Class Question Database: Psychology, 2005). For a ConcepTest to be most effective, the question must require higher-level thinking about a concept so students aren't simply recalling something they read or using "plug-and-chug" with equations. Questions must also be at an appropriate difficulty level so students are challenged but can reason to the answer with their existing knowledge.

To choose the best ConcepTests, instructors need to gauge what concepts are causing student difficulties and what level of question is appropriate for their class. By assigning JiTT assignments before class, instructors receive important feedback on their students' knowledge and understanding of the material, enabling them to better prepare for a PI lecture. Reading student responses helps instructors learn what difficulties students have, what topics students are most apprehensive about, and what concepts students understand well. Combining

JiTT with PI makes preparation for class especially efficient, as it becomes much easier to choose effective ConcepTests. Often, reading student problems or misconceptions even leads to ideas for new questions.

JiTT is not only useful for instructor preparation; it also helps students prepare for class. As Figure 3.3 shows, students get the most benefit from peer discussion when about 30–70% of the class answers the ConcepTest correctly before discussion.

Too few correct answers may indicate that students do not have enough understanding or knowledge to engage productive discussions. Therefore, students must come to class with some knowledge and ideas about the material. Often instructors administer reading quizzes at the start of class to promote pre-class reading; however, this assignment often relies solely on student memorization of facts, definitions, or equations. JiTT also encourages students to read the material, but the questions ask for more than memorization of key words and definitions and push students to start thinking more deeply about the concepts. In addition, most JiTT exercises include a question of the type, "After completing this exercise, what concepts are still unclear to you?," which promotes reflective thinking by students and provides formative feedback on students' thinking processes for instructors.

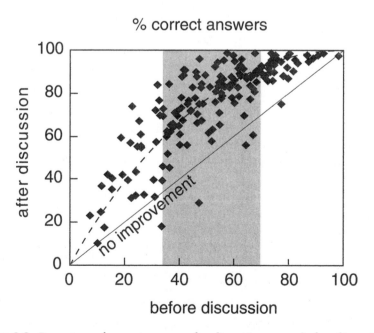

Figure 3.3. Percentage of correct answers after discussion versus before discussion. Gray area indicates optimum before-discussion percentages for the highest gain.

WHY PI PLUS JiTT WORKS

A great deal of research on cognition and learning indicates that students learn by using their existing knowledge, beliefs, and skills to create new knowledge (Bransford, Brown, & Cocking, 1999). Therefore, pedagogies in which teachers are made aware of students' incoming knowledge enhance learning. JiTT and PI provide opportunities for teachers and students to recognize background knowledge during the pre-class reading, initial vote, and discussion. The best in-class ConcepTests often take advantage of common student preconceptions or ideas about the material so students can recognize these ideas and build on them. With the constant feedback from the reading assignments and ConcepTests, the instructor can monitor student progress and help guide students to use their previously-held ideas to understand new concepts and theories. For example, in physics students may not fully understand Newton's First Law—an object in motion stays in motion unless acted on by an outside force—because of their own conflicting experiences outside the classroom sliding objects on flat surfaces involving friction. However, JiTT and PI can work together to help students first express their initial ideas and then through targeted questioning, guide them to develop more comprehensive ideas about motion that include friction. Although there are many books and papers that catalogue and describe commonly-held ideas in introductory science (e.g. Driver, Squires, Rushworth, & Wood-Robinson, 1994), JiTT is very useful in informing the instructor of these ideas before class, particularly for subjects with less research in student background knowledge. Additionally, the flexibility of a PI lecture makes it easy for instructors to spend more time on concepts that are difficult for students by giving more focused, short presentations or asking more ConcepTests. In a JiTT/PI class, instructors are paying attention to student thinking throughout the learning process.

PI provides a structured environment for students to voice their beliefs and resolve misunderstandings by talking with their peers. By working together to learn new concepts and skills in a discipline, students create a more cooperative learning environment that emphasizes learning as a community in the classroom (Hoekstra, 2008). Research suggests that this type of cooperative learning environment can help promote deeper learning, as well as greater interest and motivation (Cross, 1998). Furthermore, the strategies students use during collaboration (explaining, reasoning, and justifying arguments) can also help students develop more advanced critical thinking skills that can be used beyond the classroom (Gokhale, 1995).

Although PI can help students develop discussion skills, JiTT can help students develop skills in reading for understanding, which may be especially difficult for students when learning new, unfamiliar material. Additionally, novice learners often employ surface learning approaches that differ markedly from the deeper thinking processes of experts (Bransford et al., 1999). With JiTT, instructors can help guide students' reading by choosing questions that highlight the most important or challenging points or target deeper issues. With this guidance, students have the opportunity to become better readers as they get more directed practice with reading throughout the semester.

Research shows that experts are able to monitor and regulate their own understanding (Bransford et al., 1999). These metacognitive abilities enable experts to employ different strategies to improve their learning. PI and JiTT can help students develop better metacognitive skills, as they check their own understanding during pre-class reading and in-class questions. This is especially true when JiTT exercises include questions of the type, "What is still unclear?" These methods can help students recognize when they do not understand a concept, when they are unable to answer a JiTT question, or when they cannot give complete explanations to their peers during in-class discussion. With this formative, internal feedback, students can learn how to better assess their own understanding during the learning process. Both methods encourage students to take responsibility for their own learning, and emphasize understanding over simple task completion.

Another advantage to using JiTT in combination with PI is that both methods "personalize" the large classroom. With advances in both technology and pedagogy it is easy for instructors to connect with students and monitor their progress. JiTT and PI provide formative feedback to both students and instructors, and as we discuss later in the chapter, technology makes it even easier for instructors to respond to students individually, even in a large classroom.

Both JiTT and PI can readily be adopted for a variety of disciplines and classroom environments, and can be modified for different instructional goals. ConcepTests and JiTT questions can be tailored to individual classes and for diverse learning objectives. The modular nature of both methods means that instructors only need to use each method when and how they see fit. Reading assignments need only be given before class when necessary, and during class instructors can use as few as one question per class or as many as time allows. As such, JiTT and PI can be easily adapted to an instructor's personal style of teaching and combined with other teaching methods such as tutorials (McDermott, Schaffer, & Group, 2002), small group problem-solving (Heller, Keith, & Anderson, 1992), or lecture. It is this flexibility that makes these two methods so effective in so many classrooms.

USING JiTT AND PI: AN EXAMPLE

In this section we review a sample JiTT assignment and PI lecture to show how these two methods can be used together to help address student difficulties and deepen their understanding. Our example is from an introductory physics course at Harvard University, covering topics in electricity and magnetism, although these methods work well in a variety of disciplines.

This class met twice a week and students submitted JiTT assignments online by midnight the evening before each lecture. For this assignment students typically read a half chapter from the textbook and answered two conceptual JiTT questions and one additional question: "Please tell us briefly what *single* point of the reading you found most difficult or confusing. If you did not find any part of it difficult or confusing, please tell us what part you found most interesting." Students were graded for effort, not correctness, on these reading assignments. After the submission deadline, students could log into their accounts to see the correct answers for the first two questions as well as common questions (plus answers) from their peers. The instructor reviewed student answers before lecture, responded by email to student issues, and designed the next lecture, choosing which ConcepTests were appropriate. During the 1.5-hour-long lecture, students answered several ConcepTests, using either a wireless infrared device or their own personal wireless device, such as a cell phone, PDA, or laptop. Students' answers were recorded and students received participation credit for their responses. After lecture students could log in to review the ConcepTests as well as correct answer explanations, and the instructor could see statistics on students' answers before and after discussion.

To further illustrate how JiTT and PI complement each other, we detail one reading assignment and lecture from a one-semester course covering electricity and magnetism. We have selected a topic that was more likely to be covered in high school science courses—and therefore does not need a great deal of background knowledge—to help make this sample lecture more accessible to instructors in a variety of disciplines.

To prepare for lecture students were required to read four sections of a physics textbook covering ray optics, including topics such as transmission, reflection, absorption, refraction, dispersion, and image formation. They were then asked to answer three questions as part of their JiTT assignment:

1. Several of the figures show the paths of three so-called "principal" rays (1, 2, and 3) emitted from a light bulb and focused by a converging lens. How would you trace the path of a fourth ray emitted by the light bulb that bisects rays 1 and 2? (See Figure 3.4 for an example figure from the text.)

2. You are looking at a fish swimming in a pond. Compared to the actual depth at which the fish swims, the depth at which it appears to swim is *greater, smaller,* or *the same?*

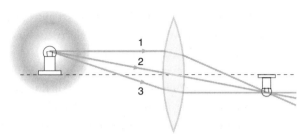

Figure 3.4. Sample Figure of Light Rays with a Converging Lens from the Text.

3. Please tell us briefly what *single* point of the reading you found most difficult or confusing. If you did not find any part of it difficult or confusing, please tell us what parts you found most interesting.

The correct answers were posted on the website for the first two questions after the assignment was due.

1. From the bulb to the lens: bisect rays 1 and 2 to find the point P where the ray strikes the lens. Then, draw a line from point P to the point where the principal rays intersect on the image of the light bulb.
2. Smaller, because at the water/air interface the light bends; the rays from the fish travel less steeply in air than in water. Therefore, the light appears to have come from a more shallow source.

Most students were able to correctly answer the first JiTT question by describing the path of a fourth ray. Students who had problems with this question often had issues with terminology or did not explicitly state how all rays would converge at the same point. Below is a sample of student JiTT responses.

- If you had a fourth ray that bisects rays 1 and 2 you would have it emerging at an angle after passing through the lens that didn't allow it to pass through the focus point. This is because it would not be paraxial and would be displaced away from the focus point.
- A fourth ray emitted by the light bulb and bisecting the angle between rays 1 and 2 should be directed through the focal point after reaching the center of the lens (so it makes a smaller angle upon reaching the center of the lens than ray 1 does, but a larger one than ray 2 makes, because ray 2 does not bend upon reaching the center of the lens).

- Well, I would probably draw it following a path that continued half way in between the other the paths followed by rays 1 and 2, but beyond that the sketch would not be very precise.

Many students answered the second JiTT question correctly, but often with sparse or incomplete explanations. Students who answered incorrectly didn't seem to grasp the concept of refraction in different mediums, especially with a flat interface. The sample student responses illustrate this point.

- The depth would be smaller due to the way the light is refracted by the water.
- The depth is the same. The water will act as a sort of lens, but because it will be a flat lens, the image size will not be changed so the fish will appear to be at the same depth.
- It obviously depends on whether the pond resembles a smooth clear lens, or a convex lens (concave doesn't really make sense here). Assuming clear/flat, the depth is the actual depth, however if the pond serves as a convex lens, no matter where the fish is it will appear as a smaller fish swimming less deep than actuality.

In addition, students wrote about their difficulties in their answer to the third JiTT reading question:

- I don't understand what a virtual image actually is. Is it literally just a trick our mind plays on us when processing visual information?
- It is difficult to conceptualize Fermat's principle in terms of the amount of time it takes light to travel. How are we supposed to know which path this is?
- I don't understand how it's possible not to see an image (as in when the object is at the focal point). Where do the light rays go? It just seems so counter-intuitive.

Students expressed difficulty or confusion on a number of different concepts. Some of these questions were best addressed by posting an answer on the website or talking about the question in class. Other student questions provided good opportunities for students to think about these concepts in class and discuss them with their neighbor.

To prepare for lecture the instructor spent a couple hours reading the student responses and reviewing the textbook and ConcepTest database to determine what additional concepts should be covered. In this particular lecture the first few ConcepTests were related to concepts about reflection, concepts that were not explicitly covered in the JiTT questions.

At the start of the lecture the instructor went over some basic logistics, including upcoming assignments and lab meetings. He then quickly summarized student responses to the JiTT assignment. As student problems were varied—spread out over many different concepts—the instructor went straight to ConcepTests to find out where students were in their understanding about the propagation of light.

The first ConcepTest (see Figure 3.5) asked about basic reflection and most students were able to answer this question correctly before discussion, indicating that they understood the idea of a virtual image formed with a mirror.

The instructor gave a short explanation and moved quickly to the next question without asking the students to discuss their answers or repolling. The second and third ConcepTests (see Figures 3.6 and 3.7) asked students to think about ray paths with reflection, which was aimed at helping students with more complex ray drawings later.

About 40% of students answered these ConcepTests correctly before discussion, while 60% of students were able to answer correctly after discussion. To help students better understand the ray paths that light takes when reflected, the instructor took some additional time to explain the concept and described examples in everyday life that might help struggling students understand. After encouraging students to review these ConcepTests again on

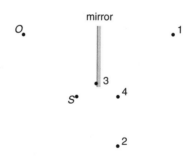

An observer O, facing a mirror, observes a light source S. Where does O perceive the mirror image of S to be located?

1. 1
2. 2
3. 3
4. 4
5. Some other location.
6. The image of S cannot be seen by O when O and S are located as shown.

Figure 3.5. First ConcepTest from Sample Lecture.

Rays of light travel from an object O to an observer at P via a reflecting surface. Which of the three paths provides the shortest path from O to P?

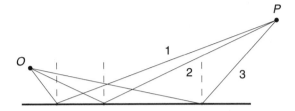

1. Path 1
2. Path 2
3. Path 3
4. All three are the same
5. The answer depends on the roughness of the surface.

Figure 3.6. Second ConcepTest from Sample Lecture.

Light enters horizontally into the combination of two perpendicular mirrors as shown below.

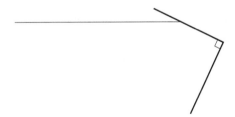

After reflecting off of both mirrors the direction of the incident light

1. bounces back and forth many times, until it hits the corner.
2. depends on the mirror angle q.
3. is reflected back and upwards.
4. is turned around by 180o.
5. is reflected back and downwards

Figure 3.7. Third ConcepTest from Sample Lecture.

their own online, the instructor moved on to talk about the speed of light through different materials. Students had additional opportunities to work with ray drawings with mirrors in the next lecture and on the homework assignment.

In their answers to the third JiTT question several students expressed confusion about Fermat's principle. After a brief reintroduction to the concept and talking about how light changes speed in different materials, the instructor posed a ConcepTest that used this principle in a more relatable context to help clear up some confusion about "least time" (see Figure 3.8).

Less than half of the students answered the ConcepTest correctly initially, but after discussing the concept with their peers, more than three-quarters of the class had a correct answer. As many students demonstrated understanding of this concept, the instructor began discussing a related concept: refraction.

A group of sprinters gather at point P on a parking lot bordering a beach. They must run across the parking lot to a point Q on the beach as quickly as possible. Which path from P to Q takes the least time? You should consider the relative speeds of the sprinters on the hard surface of the parking lot and on loose sand.

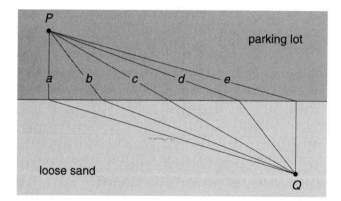

1. a
2. b
3. c
4. d
5. e
6. All paths take the same amount of time.

Figure 3.8. Fourth ConcepTest from Sample Lecture.

Based on the pre-class reading, the instructor could not be sure that students really understood the concept of refraction of light into different mediums, as many students did not give good explanations to the fish-in-water JiTT question. Therefore, the fifth ConcepTest asked students to think again about the perceived depth of the fish in the water (see Figure 3.9).

The instructor also posted a ConcepTest on the course website that phrases the question in a slightly different way, so the observer is directly over the fish. This question addresses a misconception a few students had on the reading assignment.

Looking at student answers to the pre-class reading, most students understood the basics about ray drawing with lenses. However, students needed to use these concepts for the problem set, so a series of ConcepTests were developed to probe student knowledge and advance their understanding. Due to time constraints, this lecture included only one of these ConcepTests (see Figure 3.10).

A fish swims below the surface of the water. Suppose an observer is looking at the fish from point O straight above the fish. The observer sees the fish at

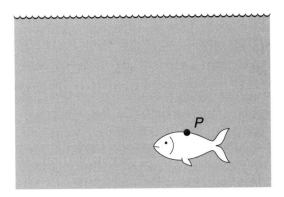

1. a greater depth than it really is.
2. the same depth.
3. a smaller depth than it really is.

Figure 3.9. Fifth ConcepTest from Sample Lecture.

Three parallel rays of light travel to the faceted piece of glass shown below. After entering the glass, the three rays

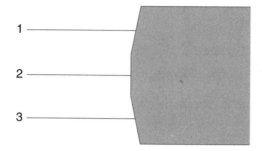

1. continue parallel.
2. converge into a point.
3. diverge.
4. other.

Figure 3.10. Sixth ConcepTest from Sample Lecture.

This particular ConcepTest helped bridge the principles of refraction to lens concepts. The next reading and lecture covered this topic more extensively.

This lecture on optics used six ConcepTests to both review material in the reading and address student difficulties. With the many resources available, the instructor was able to gauge student understanding before class, target specific areas or concepts during class, and post additional information and questions online for students to review after class. The interaction of technology and pedagogy helped streamline the work for both the instructor and students, maximizing the benefit of class time and making the classroom more personalized.

RESULTS OF USING PI AND JiTT TOGETHER

Research in physics education shows that courses incorporating "activities that yield immediate feedback through discussion with peers and/or instructors" result in greater student conceptual understanding than traditional courses (Hake, 1998). Data from introductory physics courses at Harvard University confirms this finding for PI, as seen in Figures 3.11 and 3.12.

Figure 3.11 compares results from a traditional course and several PI courses using a standardized conceptual assessment of Newtonian mechanics, the Force Concept Inventory (Hestenes, Wells, & Swackhammer, 1992). As a measure of student learning, we obtained the average normalized gain

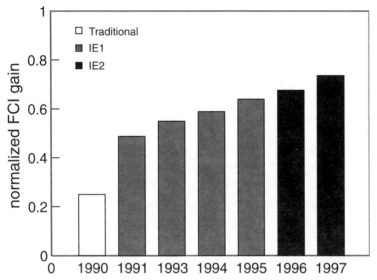

Figure 3.11. Normalized gain on the Force Concept Inventory with a traditional course (1990), IE1 courses that used PI (1991, 1993–1995), and IE2 courses that used JiTT, PI, and other interactive techniques (1996–1997). From Crouch and Mazur (2001). Reprinted with permission. © American Association of Physics Teachers.

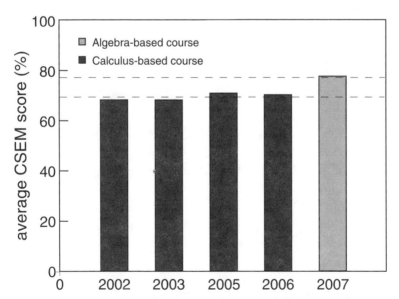

Figure 3.12. Average scores on the Conceptual Survey of Electricity and Magnetism for algebra-based and calculus-based introductory physics courses. Dotted lines represent the average scores obtained by advanced undergraduate physics majors and 2-year college professors.

(Hake, 1998) for each course, which is the gain from pretest to posttest, divided by the maximum gain possible (100% minus pretest score): $g = (post - pre)/(100 - pre)$.

As seen in Figure 3.11, PI courses (IE1) obtained greater learning gains than traditional courses. In 1996 and 1997, JiTT and tutorials were used with PI (IE2), which resulted in even higher normalized gains (Crouch & Mazur, 2001). The combination of several interactive, feedback-intensive methods, including JiTT and PI, received the highest learning gains.

Figure 3.12 shows results from introductory electricity and magnetism courses that incorporated JiTT and PI with the Conceptual Survey of Electricity and Magnetism (Maloney, O'Kuma, Hieggelke, & Van Heuvelen, 2001). The algebra-based non-major physics courses achieved average scores similar to those obtained from senior undergraduate physics students and the calculus-based course achieved an average score similar to those from two-year college physics professors (Maloney et al., 2001).

JiTT and PI not only improve conceptual learning gains of the entire class but can also help diminish gender gaps in student learning. As Figure 3.13 shows, females enter an introductory physics course at Harvard with a lower score on the Force Concept Inventory than males and this gap persists to the end of a traditional course.

With just the use of PI, the difference between males and females decreases, although the gap in posttest scores remains significant. With the use of PI, JiTT, and other interactive techniques, the gap in posttest scores is reduced even more, until males' and females' posttest scores are no longer statistically different in these introductory courses at Harvard (Lorenzo, Crouch, & Mazur, 2006). Although the results are less clear in other settings and populations (Pollock, Finkelstein, & Kost, 2007), the interactive, constructivist nature of these methods holds promise in reducing the gender gap and encouraging female students in science courses (Hazari, Tai, & Sadler, 2007; Labudde, Herzog, Neuenschwander, Violi, & Gerber, 2000; Lorenzo et al., 2006).

The increased overall learning gains with the use of PI occur not only at Harvard University. The results were replicated at a community college (Lasry, Mazur, & Watkins, 2008), indicating that PI is effective with varied student populations. Additionally, the positive results of PI are not limited to physics courses. Other studies have shown that PI is useful in improving learning in biology (Knight & Wood, 2005), engineering (Nicol & Boyle, 2003), psychology (Morling, McAuliffe, Cohen, & DiLorenzo, 2008), medicine (Rao & DiCarlo, 2000), philosophy (Bigelow, Butchart, & Handfield, 2006), and mathematics (Miller, Santana-Vega, & Terrell, 2006). Although these studies have focused on the use of PI alone, our results from adding JiTT to PI at Harvard

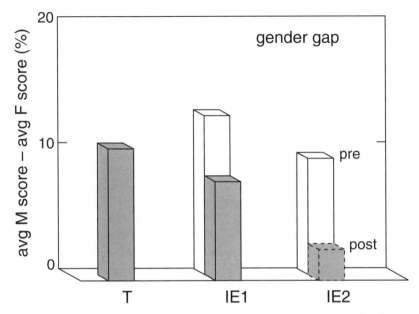

Figure 3.13. Differences in average male and average female scores on the Force Concept Inventory before and after discussion with three different pedagogies: traditional, IE1, and IE2. From Lorenzo et al. (2006). Reprinted with permission. © American Association of Physics Teachers.

suggest that students in these disciplines would similarly benefit from a combination of JiTT and PI pedagogies.

As our research has shown, combining JiTT and PI enables students to achieve greater conceptual learning gains. By exposing students to the material before class through JiTT, instructors can spend more time focusing on student understanding during class and make the classroom more centered on learning by using PI. The feedback from both methods allows instructors to adapt to their students' needs and personalize their interactions. During class, students can use their ideas developed during pre-class reading to interact with their peers and become active participants in their own learning. As a result, both instructors and students are more connected and learn more from each other, even in the largest courses.

USING PI AND JiTT WITH THE INTERACTIVE LEARNING TOOLKIT (ILT)

JiTT and PI are particularly advantageous in providing formative feedback to the instructor about students' understanding. Figure 3.14 shows a schematic

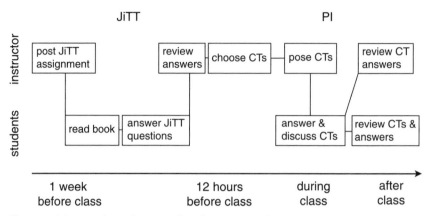

Figure 3.14. Timeline of JiTT and PI for a Given Class.

on how these methods work together, emphasizing the role of technology in providing structure and feedback throughout the learning process.

Various commercial and open-source course management systems such as Blackboard and Moodle are available to help administer JiTT to students. At Harvard University, however, we use the Interactive Learning Toolkit, (ILT, http://www.deas.harvard.edu/ilt) which helps implement both JiTT and PI, in addition to traditional course management features. The ILT includes reading and lecture modules, as well as a database of ConcepTests and a ConcepTest creation tool.

For JiTT, the reading module provides features to help create and announce reading assignments. Students complete the assignment online by a given due date. Instructors and teaching assistants are able to quickly review all student responses to a given question, revealing common weaknesses in the class's understanding (see Figure 3.15). The ILT also permits instructors to respond to questions or difficulties expressed in student responses via a labor-saving web interface, increasing students' sense of individual connection to the instructor.

With PI, use of electronic devices such as "personal response systems" (clickers) is helpful, although not necessary, for successful implementations (Lasry, 2008). Many instructors use simple hand-raising or flashcards to poll their students (Fagen, 2003). However, hand-raising allows students to see how their peers vote, which may bias their responses. Flashcards keep students' responses private from their peers and results show that flashcards work just as well as technological polling methods (i.e., handheld devices) in improving student learning (Lasry, 2008). Although it is not necessary for implementation of PI, technology can be very useful to instructors, as students can submit their answers to ConcepTests electronically, giving precise,

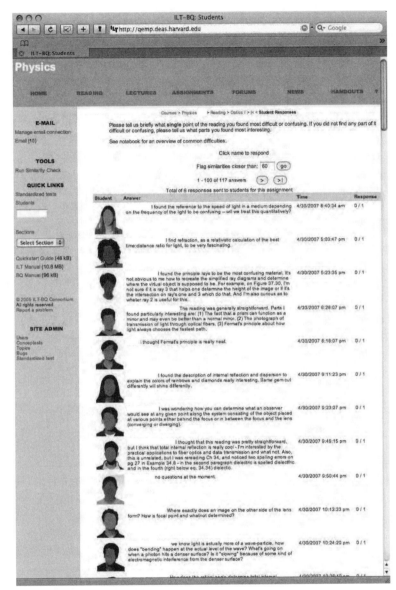

Figure 3.15. Screenshot of JiTT Reading Responses from Instructor's Viewpoint on ILT.

real-time feedback. In addition, students can use wireless handheld devices, clickers, or more recently, personal wireless devices such as cell phones, PDAs, or laptops. With these devices instructors can collect data on student performance in class and longitudinal data on individual students. Additionally, advances in technology have allowed for the creation of seating maps with students' responses, enabling instructors to focus their attention on groups of struggling students during their discussions.

In addition to helping coordinate the JiTT reading assignments, the ILT contains a searchable ConcepTest database, with over 800 physics questions, many developed at other institutions for either algebra- or calculus-based introductory physics, and some developed for non-introductory courses. Users can generate class-ready materials, such as pages for a course website or overheads for class, directly from the database. Links to separate databases of ConcepTests for astronomy and chemistry are also available. Lectures can be used to design PI classes and are linked by dates and times. With the database of ready-to-use ConcepTests the instructor can choose which conceptual questions best probe students' understanding. Additionally, the ILT provides an easy way to create additional ConcepTests in .pdf format, which can also be shared and added to the database. The instructor can easily generate a set of ConcepTests for a given lecture topic and post these for students to access after class.

If the instructor uses an electronic response system to poll students for answers to in-class ConcepTests, the lecture module of the ILT contains a feature to record student responses and statistics for each question (see Figure 3.16).

The ILT also links student answers with other aspects of the course, such as performance on pre-class reading, assignments, and exams. Additionally, we have integrated the technology of the ILT with *Beyond Question* (Junkin, 2008), which allows students to use wireless-enabled devices, such as cell phones, laptops, or PDAs to respond to in-class ConcepTests. With many students already using these devices in class, this feature alleviates the need for students to purchase an additional device and reduces the technical infrastructure needed in the classroom.

Standardized tests, including those mentioned in this article, are also available on the ILT and can be provided to students as online assignments. These tests are designed to assess students' conceptual understanding, quantitative problem-solving skills, or attitudes about undergraduate science courses, and can be taken pre- and post-course to provide information on the effectiveness of the instruction in these specific areas. The database of these tests is growing, and currently includes the Force Concept Inventory (Hestenes et al., 1992), Mechanics Baseline Test (Hestenes & Wells, 1992), Astronomy Diagnostic Test (Hufnagel et al., 2000), Conceptual Survey on Electricity and Magnetism (Maloney et al., 2001), Lawson's Test of Scientific Reasoning (Lawson, 1978), and the Maryland Physics Expectations Survey (Redish, Saul, & Steinberg, 1998). Other standardized tests can be easily added to the database. The ILT software is freely available to any interested instructor, requiring only that the instructor register at http://www.deas.harvard. edu/ilt.[1]

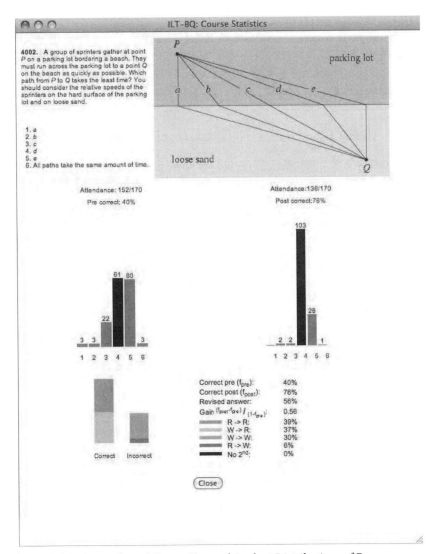

Figure 3.16. Screenshot of ConcepTest and Student Distributions of Responses, as Displayed on the ILT.

CONCLUSION

Just-in-Time Teaching and Peer Instruction work well together to advance and deepen student understanding, provide feedback to students and faculty, and help the instructor make better use of class time. By shifting students' first exposure to the material to before class, time spent in class is better used on more difficult concepts and to extend students' understanding and analysis of the concepts they already understand. Moreover, both pedagogies give formative feedback to the professor and to the students, which helps the professor tailor her/his instruction and gives students an opportunity to monitor their own learning. PI and JiTT, used together, are easy to implement in a variety of classroom settings and disciplines, and the results so far are promising for improving student learning.

Note

1. In order to preserve the security of standardized tests such as the Force Concept Inventory an instructor must also send email to galileo@deas.harvard.edu in order to gain access to these tests.

References

Bigelow, J., Butchart, S., & Handfield, T. (2006). *Evaluations of peer instruction.* Retrieved May, 2008, from http://arts.monash.edu.au/philosophy/peer-instruction/ evaluations/index.php

Bigelow, J., Butchart, S., & Handfield, T. (2007). *Peer instruction question database.* Retrieved May, 2008, from http://arts.monash.edu.au/philosophy/peer-instruction/ database/index.php

Bransford, J. D., Brown, A. L., & Cocking, R. R. (1999). *How people learn: Brain, mind, experience and school.* Washington, D.C.: National Academy of Science.

Canadian in-class question database: Psychology. (2005). Retrieved May, 2008, from http://cinqdb.physics.utoronto.ca/questions/psychology/

Cross, K. P. (1998). Why learning communities? Why now? *About Campus 3*(3), 4–11.

Crouch, C. H., Fagen, A., Callan, J. P., & Mazur, E. (2004). Classroom demonstrations: Learning tools or entertainment? *American Journal of Physics, 72*(6), 835–838.

Crouch, C. H., & Mazur, E. (2001). Peer instruction: Ten years of experience and results. *American Journal of Physics, 69*(9), 970–977.

Crouch, C. H., Watkins, J., Fagen, A., & Mazur, E. (2007). Peer instruction: Engaging students one-on-one, all at once. In E. F. Redish & P. Cooney (Eds.), *Reviews in Physics Education Research, 1*(1). Retrieved May, 2008 from http://www. percentral.org/per_reviews/volume1.cfm

Draper, S., Cargill, J., & Cutts, Q. (2002). Electronically enhanced classroom interaction. *Australian Journal of Educational Technology, 18*(1), 13–23.

Driver, R., Squires, A., Rushworth, P. & Wood-Robinson, V. (1994). *Making sense of secondary science: Research into children's ideas.* London: Routledge.

Ellis, A. B., Cappellari, A., Lisensky, G. C., Lorenz, J. K., Meeker, K., Moore, D., Campbell, K., Billmann, J., & Rickert, K. (2000). *ConcepTests.* Retrieved May, 2008, from http://www.jce.divched.org/JCEDLib/QBank/collection/ConcepTests/

Fagen, A. (2003). *Assessing and enhancing the introductory science course in physics and biology: Peer instruction, classroom demonstrations, and genetics vocabulary.* Cambridge: Harvard University Press.

Gokhale, A. (1995). Collaborative learning enhances critical thinking. *Journal of Technology Education, 7*(1), 22–30.

Green, P. (2002). *Peer instruction for astronomy.* Upper Saddle River: Prentice Hall.

Hake, R. R. (1998). Interactive-engagement versus traditional methods: A six-thousand student survey of mechanics test data for introductory physics courses. *American Journal of Physics, 66*(1), 64–74.

Hazari, Z., Tai, R., & Sadler, P. (2007). Gender differences in introductory university physics performance: The influence of high school physics preparation and affective factors. *Science Education, 91*(6), 847–876.

Heller, P., Keith, R., & Anderson, S. (1992). Teaching problem solving through cooperative grouping. Part 1: Group versus individual problem solving. *American Journal of Physics, 60*(7), 627–636.

Hestenes, D., & Wells, M. (1992). A mechanics baseline test. *The Physics Teacher, 30*(3), 159–166.

Hestenes, D., Wells, M., & Swackhammer, G. (1992). Force concept inventory. *The Physics Teacher, 30*(3), 141–158.

Hoekstra, A. (2008). Vibrant student voices: exploring the effects of the use of clickers in large college courses. *Learning, Media and Technology, 33*(4), 329-341.

Hufnagel, B., Slater, T. F., Deming, G., Adams, J. P., Adrian, R. L., Brick, C., & Zeilik, M. (2000). Pre-course results from the astronomy diagnostic test. *Publications of the Astronomical Society of Australia, 17*(2), 152–155

Hughes-Hallett, D., Gleason, A. M., McCallum, W. G., Flath, D. E., Lock, P. F., Tucker, T. W., Lomen, D. O., Lovelock, D., Mumford, D., Osgood, B. G., Quinney, D., Rhea, K., & Tecosky-Feldman, J. (2005). *ConcepTests.* New York: John Wiley & Sons.

Junkin, W. *Beyond Question.* Retrieved May, 2008, from http://www.erskine.edu/bq/

Knight, J. K., & Wood, W. B. (2005). Teaching more by lecturing less. *Cell Biology Education, 4*(4), 298–310.

Labudde, P., Herzog, W., Neuenschwander, M. P., Violi, E., & Gerber, C. (2000). Girls and physics: teaching and learning strategies tested by classroom interventions in grade 11. *International Journal of Science Education, 22*(2), 143–157.

Landis, C. R., Ellis, A. B., Lisensky, G. C., Lorenz, J. K., Meeker, K., & Wamser, C. C. (2001). *Chemistry ConcepTests: A pathway to interactive classrooms.* Upper Saddle River: Prentice Hall.

Lasry, N. (2008). Clickers or flashcards: Is there really a difference? *The Physics Teacher, 46*(4), 242–245.

Lasry, N., Mazur, E., & Watkins, J. (2008). Peer instruction: From Harvard to community colleges. *American Journal of Physics, 76*(11), 1066-69.

Lawson, A. E. (1978). The development and validation of a classroom test of formal reasoning. *Journal of Research in Science Teaching, 15*(1), 11–24.

Lorenzo, M., Crouch, C. H., & Mazur, E. (2006). Reducing the gender gap in the physics classroom. *American Journal of Physics, 74*(2), 118–122.

Maloney, D. P., O'Kuma, T. L., Hieggelke, C. J., & Van Heuvelen, A. (2001). Surveying students' conceptual knowledge of electricity and magnetism. *American Journal of Physics, 69*(7/Suppl), S12–S23.

Mazur, E. (1997). *Peer instruction: a user's manual.* Upper Saddle River: Prentice Hall.

McDermott, L. C., Schaffer, P. S., & University of Washington Physics Education Group. (2002). *Tutorials in Introductory physics.* Upper Saddle River: Prentice Hall.

Miller, R. L., Santana-Vega, E., & Terrell, M. (2006). Can good questions and peer discussion improve calculus instruction? *Primus, 16*(3), 193–203.

Morling, B., McAuliffe, M., Cohen, L., & DiLorenzo, T. (2008). Efficacy of personal response systems ("clickers") in large introductory psychology classes. *Teaching of Psychology, 35*(1), 45–50.

Nicol, D. J., & Boyle, J. T. (2003). Peer instruction versus class-wide discussion in the large classes: A comparison of two interaction methods in the wired classroom. *Studies in Higher Education, 28*(4), 457–474.

Pollock, S. J., Finkelstein, N. D., & Kost, L. E. (2007). Reducing the gender gap in the physics classroom: How sufficient is interactive engagement? *Physical Review Special Topics - Physics Education Research, 3* (010107), 4 pages.

Rao, S., & DiCarlo, S. (2000). Peer instruction improves performance on quizzes. *Advances in Physiology Education, 24*(1), 51–55.

Redish, E. F., Saul, J. M., & Steinberg, R. N. (1998). Student expectations in introductory physics. *American Journal of Physics, 66*(3), 212–224.

Starting point—Teaching entry level geoscience: ConcepTest examples. (2008). Retrieved May, 2008, from http://serc.carleton.edu/introgeo/interactive/ctestexm.html

Terrell, M. (2005). *GoodQuestions Project.* Retrieved May, 2008, from http://www.math.cornell.edu/~GoodQuestions/

Sokoloff, D. & Thornton, R. (1997). Using interactive learning demonstrations to create an active learning environment. *AIP Conference Proceedings, 399*, 1061–1074.

4

Just-in-Time Teaching in Combination With Other Pedagogical Innovations

Mark H. Maier and Scott P. Simkins

Research on teaching innovations suggests that there is potential for considerable synergy between different active learning techniques; that is, the impact on student learning of combining different types of pedagogy is often greater than the sum of the impacts of each individual pedagogical practice (Pollock, 2006; Felder, Felder, & Dietz, 1998). From its inception, Just-in-Time Teaching (JiTT) has been a pedagogy used in conjunction with other innovative teaching techniques. In the 1990s, simply using the web to assign and submit JiTT exercises was itself novel. However, as JiTT's underlying web-based structure became more commonplace, other pedagogical complementarities became evident, especially in-class teaching strategies that used students' responses to JiTT exercises as the basis for departure. In this chapter we review opportunities for using JiTT in combination with a variety of other teaching strategies and use examples, primarily from our own economics courses, but with natural extensions to other disciplines, to illustrate these complementarities. We begin with specific techniques used to write JiTT questions and then look at strategies for developing effective in-class activities informed by students' responses to these JiTT questions.

WRITING EFFECTIVE JiTT QUESTIONS

As noted throughout this book, the growing scientific literature on how students learn provides valuable guidance for developing JiTT questions that promote deep and long-lasting student learning. In particular, results from learning sciences research (see Bransford, Brown, & Cocking, 2000, p. 14–18) suggest that we:

(1) teach subject matter in depth and in a structured manner to promote expert-like thinking;

(2) uncover, understand, and work with students' preexisting knowledge, including pre- and misconceptions; and

(3) help students become self-monitoring and reflective learners.

Below we identify two pedagogies, context-rich problems and writing-across-the-curriculum techniques, as especially effective for incorporating these learning principles in JiTT exercises.[1]

USING THE *CONTEXT-RICH PROBLEM APPROACH* TO DEVELOP JiTT EXERCISES

In most disciplines, a key undergraduate learning objective is to "learn to think like an expert" in that discipline—whether learning marginal analysis in economics, use of empirical evidence in the social sciences, or understanding the scientific method in biology, chemistry, or physics. However, many university educators, especially those in science, technology, engineering, and math (STEM) fields, worry that student learning is often reduced to identifying the appropriate formula and simply inserting the correct numbers to get the required answer—usually referred to as the "plug and chug" method. As a result, these educators argue, many students maintain a novice understanding of their field as simply a search for "right" answers, disconnected from the important underlying concepts.

Unfortunately, these novice-like views of the world (and the discipline) often remain hidden to instructors, who typically use formulaic, rather than conceptual, problems to assess student learning, perpetuating the problem. The structure of many college textbooks also further retards the development of expert-like reasoning. Chapters often stand in isolation from each other so that students fail to see the connections between ideas and concepts. As one student told us recently, "I knew the answer because it was a chapter 9 problem." Finally, in most courses, regardless of discipline, students are not typically required to solve problems in different contexts or with metacognitive understanding, key elements noted above for long-lasting learning.

The context-rich problem approach. To address these common impediments to student learning, physics education researchers at the University of Minnesota (Heller, Keith, & Anderson, 1992; Heller & Hollabaugh, 1992) formulated the context-rich problem approach in the early 1990s.[2] Although initially developed for physics education (as was Just-in-Time Teaching) context-rich problems can be used in a variety of disciplines. What makes context-rich problems different from traditional problems in fields like physics, chemistry, biology, math, and economics is the intentionality in linking questions to student learning. Context-rich problems begin with "You..." and then place the student in a specific situation. For example, "You have been asked by your [roommate, boss, relative, etc.] to complete a task [helping write a novel, explain why something happens in the home, consult with a moviemaking company, etc.]." Such prompts engage student interest, link to previous student experiences, and provide guidance about the type of writing needed to answer the question.

In a second step, the context-rich approach calls attention to what is included or excluded in the details following the "You..." prompt. When designing a context-rich problem, instructors consider a variety of issues, including whether the problem should:

- include a diagram (or not)
- include excess data (so that the student needs to select the relevant information)
- exclude information that should be common knowledge or could be calculated based on common knowledge
- specify a target variable (or not)

Intentionally developing exercises that take these points into consideration are key to designing effective context-rich problems.[3]

An economics example. Consider the following JiTT exercise inspired by the context-rich problem approach that we assign in our introductory economics course to introduce students to the concept of exchange rate determination:

> You are planning a student trip to Japan and want to inform the group about events in the U.S. economy that will cause the trip to become more expensive based on changes in the dollar/yen exchange rate. List at least three possible events, and in terms that would be understood by those in the group who have not studied economics, explain why the events will cause the trip to be more expensive than previously planned.

In this example, the problem follows the context-rich problem format, beginning with "You...." in a specific context and excluding information the student should know (categories of events that cause exchange rate movement such as income or interest rate changes). In addition, the problem requires students to recognize the need for an analytical model (supply/demand diagram for exchange rates) and think metacognitively about how they learned the model so that they can explain it to an economics novice. In addition, the exercise promotes expert-like learning by helping students structure their knowledge (listing of events that would cause a shift in the demand or supply of foreign exchange).

Although the example above illustrates how context-rich problems could be used as the basis for JiTT exercises in economics, we believe that this approach has tremendous potential for writing effective JiTT questions in a wide variety of disciplines. To introduce the approach to students, instructors might initially start with a traditional end-of-chapter textbook problem and make it more context-rich by beginning the problem with "You..." and then putting the student in a novel situation. Subsequent JiTT exercises during the course can be made more challenging by adding extraneous information to standard problems or leaving out common knowledge, eventually leading up to questions that omit the target variable and require students to develop strategies to deal with unstructured problems. Such a stepwise approach helps to scaffold the learning process for students and will ultimately help students address the types of complex questions that they will encounter as they enter the workforce.

USING THE *WRITING ACROSS THE CURRICULUM APPROACH* TO DEVELOP JiTT EXERCISES

Writing Across the Curriculum researchers point out that students often have trouble engaging actively with reading material, in particular the writing format used in most textbooks. Textbook reading is often viewed by students as authoritative, a set of ideas that students must learn (i.e. memorize), not ideas that connect with anything the students learned previously or with their previous life experiences. Novice readers (students) are not generally thinking about how to integrate new ideas presented in a textbook with their current knowledge or past experience. However, modern research on learning shows that students will learn in a deeper and more durable manner if they begin to make these types of connections as they read.

In writing JiTT exercises that help students become more engaged readers, we draw from Gerald Graff and Cathy Birkenstein's (2005) *They Say/I Say: The Moves that Matter in Academic Writing* and John C. Bean's (2001) *Engaging Ideas: The Professor's Guide to Integrating Writing, Critical Thinking, and Active Learning in the Classroom.* Both books recommend writing prompts as a way to scaffold student writing so that students see a connection between academic discourse and their own ideas. Listed below is a selection of suggested writing prompts developed in the spirit of Graff, Birkenstein, and Bean that we find particularly adaptable to JiTT exercises in a variety of disciplines.[4] In each case, students are asked to fill in the blanks with course-specific concepts and ideas.

- **What did the author want me to believe?** "Before I read this text, the author assumed I believe_____; after I finished reading this text, the author wanted me to believe _____; the author was/was not successful in changing my view. How so? Why or why not?" This prompt has obvious applicability when students read argumentative essays or articles written from a particular point of view (which may not be evident to novices in the discipline). Even for textbooks, the format helps students identify the main argument in, say, a single chapter and whether or not that argument had an effect on their thinking. Note that when students first monitor their own thinking, their responses to JiTT questions like this are likely to be overly simplistic: "I didn't know that the equation for _____ was _____." In order to encourage more complex responses, it may be helpful to add to the JiTT question the first time it is used: "the author wanted me to believe _____, an important idea because _____."

- **Interview with the author.** This involves presenting a hypothetical argument against what the author has stated, then present the author's likely response to that argument. A prompt that helps students get started with this type of JiTT exercise could take the following form: "In contrast to what you have stated in this article/essay/chapter, I believe that _____ because _____." For the author's response: "I have stated things this way because _____." This type of exercise helps students to understand an argument or concept at a deeper level because they not only have to explicate the ideas being presented but also criticisms of those ideas. Student responses to this type of JiTT exercise help to identify pre/misconceptions students might have that influence their understanding of the author's words. This type of thinking would otherwise go undetected until students turn in a graded assignment or exam. A related JiTT exercise asks students to write the dialogue for a dinner party drama in which the student is seated next to the author.

- **How does the author open and close the reading?** While ideally suited for articles or essays, this simple prompt can also be adapted for a textbook, asking the student to look at a textbook reading's structure. For example: "This chapter begins with _____ because _____. The author concludes this chapter by _____ because _____." This type of JiTT exercise makes it clear that textbooks are written by authors who have a purpose for writing the chapter in a particular way, possibly linking new ideas to previously covered material or providing the groundwork for material to be presented in future chapters. In either case, it helps students to link course ideas both within and across chapters in a textbook.

- **Compare two readings.** JiTT exercises can offer a prompt that gives students a reason—perhaps an off-beat creative one—to compare two readings that differ in viewpoint or in their presentation of ideas. The following two examples illustrate what this type of prompt might look like.

  > **Example 1:** After one too many glasses of wine, Shakespeare and da Vinci have a heated debate at a dinner party about what makes a great work of art. Write the script for the dinner party debate using what you've learned about the different artists' ideas of art and culture.

  > **Example 2:** The Nobel peace prize committee has decided to, retroactively, award the prize to a scholar from the past who is now dead. They are going to pick between Scholar X (because of her invention of Z, her groundbreaking novel K, or her ability to facilitate peace between countries P and Q) and Scholar Y (because of her invention of V, her groundbreaking novel M, or her ability to facilitate peace between countries N and O). Narrate the conversation between the committee members as they debate the merits of each potential prize recipient.[5]

As these examples indicate, this type of JiTT exercise may not directly refer to the readings but puts the students in a position where they need to use the ideas presented in the readings to make a case for a decision, a point of view, or a particular idea in a novel way.

- **Creative metaphor.** This prompt asks students to come up with a metaphor that is not used in the textbook: "_____ is like _____, but _____ is like _____." In our courses we use prompts such as the following as the basis for JiTT exercises: "The difference between automatic stabilizers and discretionary fiscal policy is similar to _____." or "The difference between average cost and marginal cost is similar to_____." Peter Elbow (1981) and John Bean (2001, pp. 111–112) have explored ways in which this metaphor game can also lead to informed class discussion.

INCORPORATING JUST-IN-TIME TEACHING IN LECTURE-BASED COURSES

Experts on teaching (see, for example, Bligh (2000), Davis (2009), McKeachie and Svinicki (2005), and Nilson (2007)) agree that effective lectures do the following:

- Begin with a "hook" to pique student interest
- Connect new ideas to student experience and previous thinking
- Stop periodically so that students and the lecturer can assess what has been learned

The Just-in-Time Teaching strategy is designed to help with each of these recommendations. In addition, incorporating JiTT in traditional lecture-based courses increases student engagement and provides instructors with valuable formative assessment information about student learning—which in turn can be used to develop in-class exercises and out-of-class assignments that target specific learning difficulties identified in students' responses to JiTT exercises. Below we illustrate how JiTT can be effectively integrated into lecture-based courses, even those with class sizes of hundreds of students.

Using students' JiTT responses at the start of class. JiTT practitioners often use student responses as a way to begin class, typically displaying a small group of responses (anonymously) as class begins as a way to signal the day's topic and to encourage and focus student conversation. Typically, instructors are able to sort students' responses into groups based on common conceptual, problem-solving, or informational mistakes. The responses displayed to the class are representative samples from these groups. These responses, in turn, can be used with a compelling over-arching question such as "Which of these responses is best? Why?" or "How could these responses be combined to develop a more complete answer?" Such discourse lets students know in a formative way that the responses are incomplete and require further refining. Starting class in this way gets students much more engaged than beginning a class by lecturing on a topic or even using the responses to show "the right answer."

Using JiTT responses at the start of class completely changes the tone of the class. Students readily engage when they believe their work is an integral part of the class. In addition, students appreciate the fact that instructors are intentionally focusing on conceptual challenges and difficulties identified in their responses prior to "counting" on a high-stakes exam. The displayed responses can be used in a variety of ways: to highlight particularly novel or humorous answers, to emphasize common errors in analysis, or simply to show the quality of work that is expected in JiTT submissions (and by extension, in the course).

As we have emphasized elsewhere (chapter 8, this volume) it is important to let students know at the beginning of the semester (via the syllabus, for example) that their responses to JiTT exercises will be used in class. That said, we avoid using highly personal or possibly embarrassing responses and make an effort to rotate which students are featured. No student has ever objected to our use of her/his work; in fact, more common is a sense of pride and public claims of attribution ("Hey, that's my answer!") even when the illustrated responses reflect conceptual errors.

Opening class with a sample of students' JiTT responses provides a valuable segue into group-based activities that allow all students to participate in the solution-generating process, rather than launching into a lecture or putting students to work on a task where no starting point has been provided. We've all had this experience as faculty members in committee work—it's much more difficult to generate ideas or solutions from "scratch" than to have someone's (or in this case, a number of people's) draft to edit, critique, and respond to.

Using students' JiTT responses during a lecture. One benefit of the JiTT approach is that lectures themselves can be interspersed with examples of student responses. Most commonly, we hear that instructors illustrate key points with student examples, which are often more varied, timely, and appropriate than those the instructor is likely to use. In addition, student writing can be used in a constructivist sense: "Here's what many of you considered as you tackled this new topic," or "Here are two different responses. Let's think about why you reached different conclusions." Using a similar approach, philosopher Steve Bie (Glendale Community College, California) draws on student responses to a modern-day ethical problem ("your bank mistakenly credits your account") to illustrate arguments he will present by a classical thinker. He then asks students to think how they would modify their argument on this present-day problem after hearing the thoughts of the classical thinker.

In recent years instructors in many disciplines have begun to use multiple-choice "ConcepTest" questions in conjunction with personal response systems (clickers) to promote active student engagement in lecture-based courses.[6] Typically these questions are embedded in digital presentations and used every 10–15 minutes during a lecture to assess student learning of material being presented. Although in-class use of ConcepTest questions varies across instructors,

Eric Mazur and his colleagues at Harvard University (Crouch, Fagen, Callan, & Mazur, (2004); Crouch & Mazur, (2001); Mazur (1997)) have found that when used in conjunction with "peer instruction," a specific form of cooperative learning, ConcepTests are capable of producing significant learning gains among physics students. More recently, Mazur has begun to use JiTT as an out-of-class complement to the in-class ConcepTest/peer instruction strategy to further boost student learning (see Watkins & Mazur, chapter 3). Students' responses to JiTT questions provide valuable pre-class formative assessment that informs the development of in-class ConcepTest questions. As noted by Watkins & Mazur, the one-two punch has increased student learning beyond that achieved by ConcepTests/peer instruction alone. We believe that similar learning gains can be achieved in many disciplines by intentionally linking JiTT with ConcepTests and peer instruction. The underlying focus of this pedagogical combination—generating more active learning, even in large lecture sections; increasing students' responsibility for learning; providing immediate formative assessment on student learning; and reducing the reliance on passive lecturing—is universally applicable.

USING JiTT RESPONSES TO PROMOTE IN-CLASS COOPERATIVE LEARNING

JiTT adopters often use in-class small group work as a follow-up to out-of-class JiTT exercises. In our experience, this type of teaching practice works best when informed by the research findings on classroom use of cooperative learning.[7] This literature recommends group sizes of 2–4 students with heterogeneous skill levels and backgrounds, organized by the instructor so that friends don't work together.[8] In addition, group work needs to be well structured so that students can function on learning rather than second-guessing what they should be doing. Ideally, this structure requires each student to have a clearly-defined and purposeful role in group work (note-taker, time-keeper, summarizer, etc.). In addition, group work should include a mechanism for enforcing individual accountability to reduce problems with free-riding.

Several specific techniques are available to incorporate in-class cooperative learning in conjunction with JiTT exercises. Below we summarize a number of the most widely-used techniques.[9]

Think-Pair-Share

The easiest way to adapt JiTT exercises for group work in class, and likely the most commonly-used, is the think-pair-share technique. Think-pair-share can be initiated on-the-spot, perhaps when student attention appears to be waning during a lecture, or can be prearranged based on information revealed in students' JiTT responses. When used at the beginning of class in conjunction with a set of projected JiTT responses, instructors can quickly ask students to break into pairs, employing the think-pair-share strategy to determine which answer is best, identify errors, or suggest modifications that would improve the responses. Students first consider the question and answer it individually, then consult with a nearby classmate.

The ConcepTest/peer instruction technique described earlier is a special case of think-pair-share, with students responding individually using colored cards or personal response systems (clickers), then consulting with a classmate before responding again, with the distribution of responses in each case shown to the class to provide formative assessment on learning. The instructor may also ask individual students to share with the class the reasoning behind their answers as a way to close the activity.

The following examples illustrate how this technique might be used in an economics course, although the examples can be easily adapted for other disciplines.

Example 1: In a JiTT exercise related to an article on international trade, the student responses may reveal confusion about the concepts of comparative advantage, free trade, and trade protection (such as the infant industry argument)—confusion that students may not even be aware of as novice learners in economics. In this case the instructor could use the responses as the basis for a think-pair-share exercise, asking students to identify specific uses of the concepts in the selected responses.

Example 2: In this example, a JiTT exercise may ask students to select and defend a particular macroeconomic policy response to recent data showing that the economy has entered a severe recession. Shown in class are four student JiTT responses, each missing some conceptual elements. In this case, the think-pair-share exercise could simply have students determine which response is "best" and why. Through a showing of cards, clicker responses, or a simple show of hands, the instructor can quickly determine the distribution of responses. If the responses are distributed across all four choices, the think-pair-share exercises could continue with multi-group discussion asking students to evaluate the four responses on the strength of the economic arguments, the accuracy of the economic concepts employed, and the use of supporting evidence.

Cooperative Controversy

In this activity, student responses to JiTT exercises submitted before class form the basis for a highly structured debate. In our experience, this format can be completed in a relatively short time period, as short as twenty minutes, and unlike standard classroom debates, allows every student to speak and explore both sides of the controversy.[10] Briefly, students are assigned by the instructor to "pro" and "con" sides in a policy debate such as "The minimum wage should be eliminated." Each pair reads JiTT responses on "their" side and summarizes in writing three different reasons to favor this position. Students then combine with a student pair on the other side and each side reports its reasons. Next, the group of four identifies the weakest and strongest reason on each side. Finally, individual students are asked to write an essay in which they present their view on the controversy. A more structured use of "oppositional readings" is illustrated by Claude Cookman in chapter 10.

Jigsaw

Jigsaw is a cooperative learning technique in which members of, say, a four-person group (the base group) first count off 1-2-3-4 and reconfigure themselves in groups with all the 1's together, all the 2's together, all the 3's together, and all the 4's together. Each of these newly-constituted groups becomes an "expert group" on a different, but complementary, concept, issue, or skill related to a common topic or theme. Once the members of the expert group have achieved their "expert" status (by reading an article, looking up information on the web, practicing a skill, etc.) the original base groups reconvene so that each group now has an "expert" in one of the four designated areas. Members in each group share their expertise with the other group members so that all group members are briefed on each of the four areas highlighted in the activity.

To highlight how the jigsaw technique might be used in conjunction with JiTT exercises, consider the following example that is a slight modification of the process described above: The pre-class JiTT exercise requires students to submit a letter to the editor of the local newspaper arguing in favor of increasing or decreasing a specific type of tax (e.g., income, property, sales, excise taxes). In class, students in the original (base) groups each individually choose a different tax to analyze. Students join expert groups comprised of students who chose the same tax. In the expert groups, students analyze JiTT responses related to that tax. Students then rejoin base groups and report on the tax for which they were the expert.

Gallery Walk

The gallery walk technique requires individuals or groups to first develop a one-sheet "poster" on a given topic and then post the resulting sheets around the room for public display. The posters may contain lists, ideas, suggestions, strategies, concept maps, or a variety of other types of information. After the information is posted, students working in small groups circulate around the room and comment on the posters in response to specific questions or directions developed by the instructor.

For a gallery walk example incorporating a JiTT exercise, consider the following version of the gallery walk technique: As part of a pre-class JiTT exercise students submit recommendations for dealing with "price gouging" by snow plow entrepreneurs after a snow storm. At the beginning of class selected JiTT responses are posted on the wall. Next to each response are large, blank, easel-board sized papers on which students, working in small groups, must draw a diagram to illustrate the solution recommended in the JiTT response. Groups then rotate to new posters, adding a written evaluation of the policy response and the associated diagram. After rotating multiple times, groups are asked to summarize (and possibly rank, based on effectiveness, fairness, cost, or some other criterion) the solutions that they reviewed.

USING JUST-IN-TIME TEACHING WITH CLASSROOM EXPERIMENTS

JiTTs can serve as an effective bridge between running an experiment (in or out of class) and subsequent discussion of the experimental results. This use of JiTT builds on research findings highlighting the importance of student predictions before an experiment is conducted. Research with Harvard pre-med students (Crouch et al, 2004) found that with as little as two minutes spent prior to an experiment predicting its outcome (in consultation with another student), the number of correct answers doubled and the number of correct explanations quadrupled. By making predictions, students were more self-aware of the mental model they brought to the classroom and focused their attention on the concept under study before they became engaged in the experiment. Before running in-class economics experiments in our courses we use JiTT exercises to ask students to make predictions about what will occur under specific circumstances. Predictions that differ, along with the student explanations, are presented to students before they run the experiment, focusing student attention on core concepts we want them to learn. A similar strategy can be used in any discipline that makes regular use of demonstrations, experiments, or simulations.

USING JiTT TO PREPARE STUDENTS FOR SEMINARS

To prepare for discussion seminars in small-enrollment courses, instructors typically ask students to read in advance and document their preparation with a brief essay submitted before the seminar begins or with a reading quiz at the start of class. Like these traditional approaches, JiTT pedagogy promotes student preparation for in-class discussion and makes student effort visible. In contrast, however, JiTT provides an opportunity for instructors to better monitor student misunderstandings before the classroom discussion begins. As a result, student responses to JiTT questions can provide a useful starting point for class discussion or inform the types of questions posed by the instructor during the seminar session.[11]

Henderson and Rosenthal (2006) discuss a variant of this approach in their use of "reading questions." Instead of using JiTT exercises to generate responses to instructor-developed questions, they use JiTT exercises to have students develop and submit their own "reading questions" about an article, textbook passage, or book (or simply a topic or concept covered in the course that will be the topic for discussion in the seminar) that identify areas of ongoing confusion, difficulty, or lack of understanding. These questions, especially if repeated in a number of students' responses, can be used to direct the seminar discussion in a way that ensures that student learning gaps are addressed.

CONCLUSION

In the same way that this book is only one in a series of books highlighting effective pedagogical practices, JiTT is a classroom technique that most instructors will use in combination with other innovations. Our intent in this chapter is to illustrate a wide range of teaching strategies with which JiTT can be effectively combined, to spark new ideas about how JiTT might be developed, and to show how JiTT responses might be used in the classroom to improve student engagement and learning. For example, we believe that JiTT questions are greatly enhanced—and students are less likely to be burned out by similarly-structured JiTTs—by borrowing ideas from the context-rich problem and Writing Across the Curriculum literature. Similarly, we believe that the use of JiTTs in class is enriched when combined with ConcepTests, peer instruction, and cooperative learning techniques.

The examples in this chapter are drawn from our classroom experience and are meant to be illustrative, not exhaustive. JiTT can just as easily be combined with other pedagogical techniques such as classroom assessment techniques, case studies, problem-based learning, and service learning, either as a way to help students prepare for these activities or as the source of textual content for analysis. No single pedagogy can achieve the multiple aims identified by the learning sciences (and listed at the start of this chapter) as critical for promoting sustained learning. We encourage you to think about how Just-in-Time Teaching might be intentionally combined with the pedagogical practices that you are already employing in your own classes to address these aims. Student learning is likely to be enhanced as a result.

Notes

1. Maier & Simkins (chapter 8) also discuss a variety of ideas for developing effective JiTT questions.

2. The University of Minnesota physics education research group maintains a Web site with advice and sample context-rich problems for physics. See http://groups.physics.umn.edu/physed/Research/CRP/crintro.html.

3. The context-rich problem approach also shares some of the same attributes of the "case method" of teaching (see, for example, National Center for Case Study Teaching in Science): posing a problem or decision that has no obvious answer, identifying actors who must solve the problem, requiring critical thinking and analysis to reach a decision, and providing enough information within the case (or problem) for good analysis. Also similar to context-rich problems is an approach called "Role, Audience, Format, Topic" (RAFT) used in K-12 instruction.

4. For additional examples see Maier & Simkins (chapter 8).

5. Examples from Sarah McLemore, Glendale Community College (California). Used with permission.

6. For further information on concept tests see http://serc.carleton.edu/introgeo/interactive/conctest.html, http://jchemed.chem.wisc.edu/JCEDLib/QBank/collection/ConcepTests/, http://www.flaguide.org/cat/contests/contests1.php, http://www.colorado.edu/physics/EducationIssues/cts/, and http://www.math.cornell.edu/~GoodQuestions/index.html.

7. The cooperative-learning literature is well developed. With respect to the use of cooperative learning in higher education we recommend: Millis (2010), Millis & Cottell (1998), Barkley, Cross, et al. (2005), and Johnson & Johnson (1998).

8. Cooperative learning experts note that there are exceptions to the heterogeneity recommendation. For example, at times it may be advantageous to ask high-skill students to work together. In addition, groups may function better if women or minorities are not isolated individually in a group.

9. These, along with additional collaborative learning techniques, are summarized in Barkley, Cross, & Major (2005). We provide additional economics-related examples in Maier, McGoldrick, & Simkins (2010).

10. For more on structured controversy see Millis & Cottell (1998, pp. 140–143).

11. Additional ideas for using JiTT to prepare students for seminar discussions are provided by Claude Cookman in chapter 10 and Salemi and Hansen (2007).

References

Barkley, E. F., Cross, K. P., & Major, C. H. (2005). *Collaborative learning techniques: A handbook for college faculty*, San Francisco: Jossey-Bass.

Bean, J. C. (2001). *Engaging ideas: The professor's guide to integrating writing, critical thinking, and active learning in the classroom.* San Francisco: Jossey-Bass.

Bligh, D. A. (2000). *What's the use of lectures?* San Francisco: Jossey-Bass.

Bransford, J. D., Brown, A. L., & Cocking, R. R. (Eds.). (2000). *How people learn: Brain, mind, experience, and school.* Washington, D.C.: National Academy Press.

Crouch, C. H., & Mazur, E. (2001). Peer instruction: Ten years of experience and results. *American Journal of Physics, 69*(9), 970–977.

Crouch, C. H., Fagen, A. P., Callan, J. P., & Mazur, E. (2004). Classroom demonstrations: Learning tools or entertainment? *American Journal of Physics, 72*(6), 835–838.

Davis, B. G. (2009). *Tools for teaching.* San Francisco: Jossey-Bass.

Elbow, P. (1981). *Writing with power: Techniques for mastering the writing process.* New York: Oxford University Press.

Felder, R. M., Felder, G. N., & Dietz, E. J. (1998). A longitudinal study of engineering student performance and retention. V. Comparisons with traditionally-taught students. *Journal of Engineering Education, 87*(4), 469–480.

Graff, G., & Birkenstein, C. (2005). *They say/I say: The moves that matter in academic writing.* New York: W. W. Norton.

Heller, P., & Hollabaugh, M. (1992). Teaching problem solving through cooperative grouping. Part 2: Designing problems and structuring groups. *American Journal of Physics, 60*(7), 637–644.

Heller, P., Keith, R., & Anderson, S. (1992). Teaching problem solving through cooperative grouping. Part 1: Group versus individual problem solving. *American Journal of Physics, 60*(7), 627–636.

Henderson, C., & Rosenthal, A. (2006) Reading questions: Encouraging students to read the text before coming to class. *Journal of College Science Teaching, 35*(7), 46–50.

Johnson, D. R., & Johnson, R. T. (1998). *Learning together and alone: Cooperative, competitive, and individualistic learning.* Upper Saddle River: Allyn & Bacon.

Maier, M., McGoldrick, K. & Simkins, S. (2010). Cooperative learning in economics. In B. Millis (Ed.), *Cooperative learning in higher education.* Sterling, VA: Stylus Publishers.

Mazur, E. (1997). *Peer instruction: A user's manual.* Upper Saddle River: Prentice Hall.

McKeachie W., & Svinicki, M. (2005). *McKeachie's teaching tips: Strategies, research, and theory for college and university teachers.* Florence, KY: Wadsworth Publishing.

Millis, B. J. (Ed.). (2010). *Cooperative learning in higher education.* Sterling, VA: Stylus Publishers.

Millis, B. J., & Cottell, P. G. (1998). *Cooperative learning for higher education faculty.* Phoenix: Oryx Press.

National Center for Case Study Teaching in Science. (2009.) *Case Collection.* Retrieved from http://ublib.buffalo.edu/libraries/projects/cases/ubcase.htm.

Nilson, L. B. (2007). *Teaching at its best: A research-based resource for college instructors.* San Francisco: Jossey-Bass.

Pollock, S. J. (2006). Transferring transformations: Learning gains, student attitudes, and the impact of multiple instructors in large lecture classes. Physics Education Research Conference 2005. Retrieved from: http://www.colorado.edu/physics/EducationIssues/pollock/PERC_sum05_finalrevised.pdf.

Salemi, M. K., & Hansen, W. L. (2007). Discussing economics: A classroom guide to preparing discussion questions and leading discussions. Northampton, MA: Edward Elgar Publishers.

Implementing Just-in-Time Teaching in the Disciplines

PART TWO

5

Using Just-in-Time Teaching in the Biological Sciences

Kathleen A. Marrs

In recent years, scientists and science educators have advocated that college science classrooms adopt inquiry-based active-learning strategies, even in large lecture-style classes (National Research Council, 1996; Bransford, Brown, & Cocking, 2000). Recent calls for "scientific teaching" (Alberts, 2008; Bonner, 2004; Handelsman et al., 2004) provide further support for implementing research-based teaching methods that make greater use of inquiry and active learning-based teaching. As other chapters in this volume illustrate, Just-in-Time Teaching (JiTT), theoretically grounded in the learning sciences and implemented across a wide variety of disciplines, has been particularly effective at getting students actively involved in the learning process and improving student learning. JiTT is especially valuable at promoting inquiry-based learning in science, technology, engineering, and mathematics (STEM) fields, where it has enjoyed its greatest use.

This chapter highlights the value of JiTT in improving student learning and critical thinking about fundamental biological concepts and in underscoring the relevance of biology to students' lives. The chapter first broadly describes how JiTT can be used to address learning goals in the sciences. Next, using a set of scientific reasoning attributes originally described by Arnold Arons (1979) as a guide, the chapter illustrates how to write JiTT exercises that target specific scientific reasoning capacities and build student engagement. The following section describes how JiTT exercises (and students' responses to these exercises) can be used to inform and develop effective in-class exercises that focus on students' learning gaps. In the last section, data from a group of biology courses at Indiana University Purdue University Indianapolis (IUPUI) is presented showing that JiTT helps students better prepare for class, improve their study skills, persist in the course, and learn more compared to traditional lecture-only courses.

JiTT DIRECTLY TARGETS HOW STUDENTS LEARN SCIENCE

Research on how students learn science highlights three important findings that instructors can make use of to improve student learning:

- **Learning requires active practice.** Whether modeled as inquiry-based learning, peer-led recitation sections, or problem-based learning, research clearly shows that active engagement in doing science is more effective at promoting student learning than listening to a lecture (Allen & Tanner, 2005; Bybee, 2002; Hake, 1998; National Research Council, 1996; Bransford, Brown, & Cocking, 2000; Paulson, 1999). Teaching practices that get students actively involved in scientific reasoning, simulation, and experimentation are likely to lead to larger learning gains than passive lecturing.
- **Learning is actively constructed from prior knowledge.** Research in both the learning sciences and science education indicates that in order to learn, students must actively construct new knowledge from prior knowledge (Bybee, 2002; Committee on Undergraduate Science Education, 1997; Fisher et al., 1986; Bransford, Brown, & Cocking, 2000). Teaching methods that help students intentionally relate new ideas and concepts to previous experience and knowledge are more likely to improve student learning than those that do not.
- **Learning requires prompt feedback.** Learning is best achieved when students receive frequent feedback on their current or prior knowledge so they can adjust or clarify their thinking (Rutherford and Ahlgren, 1989; Bybee, 2002; Bransford, Brown, & Cocking, 2000). Teaching methods that provide frequent and timely formative assessment help students to understand and correct learning gaps.

JiTT, through the interaction of out-of-class preparatory exercises and in-class follow-up activities, provides a valuable teaching strategy to address each of these research-based findings (Marrs, Blake & Gavrin, 2003; Marrs & Novak, 2004; Marrs & Chism, 2005). JiTT exercises, when developed with results from learning sciences research in mind, provide students with relevant active learning opportunities that promote practice with new concepts and ideas, help students connect course concepts to their lives, and encourage metacognitive thinking processes.

Using pre-class JiTT exercises to improve learning and inform teaching. As noted throughout this book, these exercises are the starting point for the JiTT process. JiTT exercises typically require students to complete a reading assignment and then submit responses to a few short questions prior to the next class, usually via a web-based course management system. Although the questions included in JiTT exercises vary widely, they often present an open-ended situation that requires the student to use prior knowledge or experience, along with the assigned reading, to develop a hypothesis about a concept or idea that will be investigated more fully in the upcoming class.

Students' JiTT responses—analyzed prior to the class—often reveal learning challenges or misconceptions about the material, providing real-time feedback for instructors. The information gained from these responses is used to develop or modify classroom activities for the next class "just-in-time." During class, student responses are used directly throughout the lecture as a framework for the day's activities and as a springboard for further discussion, greatly enhancing classroom interactivity.

Using in-class interactive lectures and small-group exercises to reinforce learning. In my course, I typically start with a brief mini-lecture, incorporating student JiTT responses in the discussion, followed by a cooperative learning exercise consisting of small group activities and discussion related to the JiTT responses. The cooperative learning activities reinforce students' learning by addressing learning difficulties uncovered by their JiTT responses. In addition, these activities encourage students to attend class and participate in group problem solving and critical thinking exercises that encourage active practice with concepts and ideas. The in-class activities are followed by a second mini-lecture during the final third of the class.[1]

Linking JiTT pedagogy to learning sciences research. You can clearly see how JiTT addresses the three teaching recommendations derived from learning sciences research listed above. JiTT encourages students to be active participants in the learning process, both in and out of class. Responses to JiTT exercises typically require students to connect new ideas or concepts to previously-learned material or prior experiences. In class, students' responses provide immediate feedback to both students and instructors on the learning process and the current level of student understanding. The "just-in-time" nature of the JiTT process allows instructors to make use of student learning challenges, made visible in students' responses to JiTT exercises, to target in-class activities where they will be most effective. Overall, JiTT engages students in the course content while promoting mastery of the subject through active learning, constructivism, and prompt feedback.

USING JiTT EXERCISES TO TARGET SCIENTIFIC REASONING CAPACITIES

Students' responses to JiTT exercises are used in three important ways: (1) to identify student beliefs, preconceptions, and prior knowledge; (2) to inform classroom instruction based on student responses, and (3) to visually display in class as a means of confronting students' preconceptions and serve as a scaffold for building new knowledge. The structure of the JiTT teaching method allows students and faculty to begin each day with the students' prior knowledge as the starting point for that day's discussion. As such, faculty can maximize the benefits of students' out-of-class time by focusing on important or challenging concepts in JiTT exercises and increase the learning outcomes of the in-class session by tailoring mini-lectures and classroom activities to the student learning difficulties made visible in the students' responses.

Step 1: Writing Effective JiTT Questions

Because JiTT exercises are often developed to uncover students' prior knowledge, JiTT questions typically focus on questions or scenarios that provoke a need to know in students' minds rather than on direct factual information found in the textbook. Writing good JiTT questions is one of the most important and challenging aspects of implementing JiTT pedagogy. Although many instructors have an intuitive sense of what makes a good JiTT question, Arnold Arons' (1979) taxonomy of reasoning attributes that faculty "commonly, tacitly, and often inappropriately assume to exist in all college students" provides a useful guide for developing JiTT questions. They are particularly helpful for developing effective JiTT questions in STEM disciplines but also have applicability across a wide variety of disciplines.

     Table 5.1 lists nine of Arons' categories of reasoning capacities that I have found particularly relevant for biology courses, in some cases slightly modified from his original phrasing. In my own courses I try to intentionally develop JiTT questions that specifically target one or more of these reasoning skills, while also incorporating important biology-related concepts. For example, a JiTT question might probe for the ability of a student to understand new terms and definitions or show students' thinking processes when dealing with a difficult concept. Other JiTT questions might probe for whether a student can draw inferences from data or translate words into written symbols or written symbols into words. For each category listed in Table 5.1 I have included an example of JiTT questions that have been used in biology courses at IUPUI. Note that while the content may differ from your course or discipline, the

Table 5.1. Nine scientific reasoning capacities outlined by Arnold Arons (1979) (with links to related JiTT biology questions).

Arons Characteristic	Examples of Related JiTT Questions	Rationale
1. Understanding new terms and definitions	What is the difference between a theory and a belief? You may want to look these terms up before answering. Be as specific as you can, and give an example of each from your own life experience.	Understanding the meaning of important words is crucial as the foundation of reading comprehension, writing ability, and understanding of course material.
2. Ability to explain the meaning of a concept, or a particular bit of jargon, in their own words	What characteristic determines whether organisms belong to the same biological species? For instance, why are Rottweilers, bulldogs, and poodles-phenotypically very different-all considered to be members of the same biological species, dogs? Why are all humans, despite our numerous phenotypic differences, considered to be one biological species?	Students may be able to rephrase an idea using terminology from their text or the web without really understanding the concept. Insisting that students use their own words makes it "OK" to phrase their idea in straightforward terms.
3. Demonstration of students' thinking processes when dealing with difficult new ideas	How do you think cells become specialized for their function? For instance, we all started our life as one single fertilized egg cell, or zygote, but within weeks of conception, we had liver cells, heart cells, brain cells, and muscle cells that were grouped into functioning organs. How does one cell give rise to many cells with many different functions?	Students often demonstrate numerous steps in their thinking skills as they analyze or evaluate a complex process. This type of question allows the faculty member to see how students progress through stages in their critical thinking process.

(*continued*)

Table 5.1. (*continued*)

Arons Characteristic	Examples of Related JiTT Questions	Rationale
4. Ability of students to see connections between the subject and their own experiences	Which gender is doing more meiosis right now—the males or the females? Or do you think men and women undergo meiosis at pretty much equal rates? What type of cell is the end product of meiosis in men? What type of cell is the end product of meiosis in women?	Relevance is a key concept in constructivism and new learning—as new information is linked to prior knowledge and experience, students are challenged to confront their own mental models of a concept to make sense of the new knowledge presented.
5. Drawing inferences from data and evidence	A protein called "p53" is a tumor suppressor protein that normally functions to find damaged DNA in the nucleus and prevent cells from going through mitosis if DNA is damaged. However, many research studies have shown evidence that smoking cigarettes causes mutations in the p53 gene in lung cells. Based on this evidence, how do you think this might play a factor in the development of lung cancer?	Formulating one's own line of reasoning when presented with data is an important step in becoming a scientist or thinking scientifically. Further discussion can lead to an examination of cause-and-effect relationships or whether variables were properly controlled.
6. Estimating: getting a feel for magnitudes	Your body does not store much ATP, but must continually resynthesize ATP from ADP every second of your life during cellular respiration. About how much ATP (in pounds) do you think you resynthesize on an average day? Explain your choice.	Requiring students to show mathematical "common sense" by quantitative reasoning, particularly in a relevant context, develops logic and problem solving skills.

7. Translating words into written symbols and written symbols into words	One of my favorite quotes about biology refers to photosynthesis: "Life is woven out of air by light" (Jacob Moleschott). Look at the chemical equation for photosynthesis is this week's readings. In your own words, explain what you think the author of this quote meant based on the chemical reaction for photosynthesis.	Transforming a verbal statement into its equivalent arithmetical, algebraic, or graphical form, and vice versa, develops a biology student's ability to think and write fluently in the language of mathematics and science.
8. Relating biology to "common sense"	If we were ever to clone a person, like Albert Einstein, a brilliant physicist, do you think we would end up with another brilliant physicist? Why or why not?	Often, the fantastical scenarios presented by the popular media ("cloned" armies or dinosaurs, for instance) provide entertainment but are outside of scientific experience. Questions of this type are useful to help students develop a healthy skepticism when presented with such interesting, but unlikely, scientific possibilities.
9. To use as springboard to discuss the ethical implications of biology	Where do Human Embryonic Stem Cells (hES cells) come from? What are some of the ethical implications of using hES cells for medical research? In your opinion, explain whether you feel the potential medical benefits of hES cells justify their use in medical research, given the source of these cells.	New techniques in biology (embryonic stem cells, genetically modified crops, the human genome project) raise new questions about the ethical, legal, and social implications (ELSIs) of biology. Biology students, majors, and non-majors become informed citizens by wrestling with the ELSIs of their times.

prompts or starting phrases are universally helpful. The rationale for using these types of questions (included in the last column of Table 5.1) comes both from Arons' own words as well as my interpretations of his categories.

Step 2: Using JiTT Responses and Cooperative Learning in Class

How are students' JiTT responses used during a typical class to provide formative assessment and to guide classroom lecture/discussion? Usually, students' JiTT responses are shown at the beginning of class to spark discussion. However, in most biology courses, especially at the introductory level, there are simply too many students to provide individual feedback to JiTT responses or to show them all, so a representative sample of responses are chosen for presentation in class based on patterns that emerge from the students' submissions. Incomplete or partially correct answers are great discussion starters and can usually be extended through additional questioning of students, either as a whole class or in small groups. An extensive list of potential questions to use with students' JiTT responses is provided in Table 1.2 (chapter 1). Instructors who use JiTT note that students really enjoy seeing their actual JiTT responses shown in class and find it quite fun to provide a nickname that identifies their response (such as "Charles Darwin" or "WannaBeeMD"). While this is certainly not a necessary part of a JiTT exercise, it does provide a personal touch that increases student engagement.

Students in a JiTT classroom not only benefit by expanding, extending, and debating JiTT responses, but also by working in cooperative learning groups to engage in class-based interactive engagement activities related to the JiTT exercise. In-class activities are chosen to give students hands-on experience with specific concepts introduced in the JiTT exercise (for example, transcription and translation using the codon chart, genetics problems, or graphing exercises to show exponential population growth or antibiotic resistance) or to respond to a learning challenge identified in the JiTT responses.[2] Listed below are two general examples of how JiTT questions and in-class cooperative learning activities can be intentionally linked to reinforce student learning.

Example #1:

JiTT Question: Starch (like bread or pasta) is a glucose polymer that gives us energy, but cellulose, an almost identical glucose polymer, is indigestible. Why do you think that one of these almost identical molecules can be digested, while the other can't? Why is cellulose (non-nutritive and indigestible) a very necessary part of our diet?

In-class Activity: Conduct a cooperative learning exercise giving students practice with condensation reactions that join monomers to make polymers, then link back to student responses from the JiTT activity.

Example #2:

JiTT Question: If you and your spouse are carriers for sickle cell disease (Ss), you have a 25% chance (1 in 4 chance) of producing a child with sickle cell disease. If you have 4 children, does this mean that one of then will have sickle cell disease? Why or why not?

In-class Activity: Develop and implement a hands-on cooperative learning exercise using Punnitt Squares and probability calculations in determining genetic outcomes to reinforce the concepts introduced in the JiTT question.

In my introductory biology classes, informal groups of two to four students work together for 10–15 minutes on these cooperative activities and are given time to ask questions and discuss their answers with other groups. Although students are sometimes hesitant at the beginning of the semester to work with other students, they quickly come to enjoy the break in lecture and welcome the chance to practice working with concepts that we are discussing in class. A vast majority of students report that the cooperative learning exercises are very helpful in promoting their understanding of course concepts.

We have also found additional benefits of the cooperative learning exercises that are not directly related to facilitating understanding of course content. One is that the cooperative learning exercises foster in-class student-to-student interaction and many times result in the formation of study groups outside of class, an important factor for student success that is often difficult to establish on an urban campus. A second is that the cooperative learning exercises strongly promote classroom attendance, particularly if an attendance sheet is signed and used to award a small number of points. More than 85% of the class is regularly in attendance throughout the semester when cooperative learning exercises are used, a figure almost double what was experienced before cooperative learning exercises were implemented in our biology courses.

WHAT IS BIOLOGY GOOD FOR? EXTENDING THE CLASSROOM EXPERIENCE

Biology is possibly the most rapidly advancing branch of science today. Cell biology alone has seen an impressive increase recently in the knowledge about signal transduction, protein sorting, regulation of gene expression, cell division, and molecular genetics. Obviously, not all of these topics can become part of the curriculum. However, faculty may feel that a certain topic could really be beneficial or interesting to those students motivated enough to want to go a little more in-depth than the curriculum permits. To introduce these extracurricular topics and enhance student motivation, our JiTT approach uses a final optional assignment, called *What is (Biology) Good For?*[3] Each week a new essay is posted. The *Good For* essays provide a reasonable introduction to a discipline-related topic, typically contained in one thousand words or less and a few figures, followed by three research questions for which students may earn a small amount of extra credit. The extra credit points (along with the compelling nature of the essays) are enough to achieve considerable participation. We have found at IUPUI that over 75% of the students regularly submit responses to the optional *Good For* essays.

The *Good Fors* are written to provide a clear sense of the excitement of modern biology by directly linking material in the text to a practical application of biology upon which lives may depend. The research questions at the end of the essays require students to do a bit of guided Internet research using links included throughout the body of the essay or in a set of "further reading" links at the end. The goal is to activate the students' interest and the idea that biology occupies a central position in their lives. Ideally, students begin to tune into news stories about biology in their everyday lives, something that is not hard to do these days with almost daily news stories about human embryonic stem cells, cloning, or the human genome project. The *Good For* essays have the additional effect of promoting science literacy, requiring students to practice their writing skills, and helping students gain experience using the Web as a resource. Similar resources have also been developed for physics and chemistry classes at IUPUI (Gavrin & Novak, 1999; Gavrin, Marrs, Black, & Watt, 2000).

HOW DOES JiTT AFFECT STUDENTS' LEARNING AND STUDY HABITS?

JiTT has been used in three types of biology courses at IUPUI over the past decade: (1) a large-enrollment, no-lab, lecture hall course for non-science majors; (2) a large-enrollment lecture hall course with both a weekly lab and a peer-led recitation associated with the lecture, typically taken by freshman with pre-professional interests in medicine, pharmacy, dentistry, or other health-related careers; and (3) an advanced level topics course taken mainly by graduate students. In total, over 6,000 biology students at IUPUI have been taught using JiTT. What have we learned from our experience? As the JiTT strategy is designed to encourage both attitudinal and cognitive gains among participants, our assessment efforts have been focused on measuring JiTT's impact in three areas: (1) student study skills; (2) course attrition rates; and (3) students' cognitive gains as reflected in student performance on achievement tests and end-of-semester course grades. Results from each of these areas are presented below.

JiTT Improves Class Preparation

To make the best use of in-class time, most instructors would agree that it is important for students to come to class prepared. In a JiTT classroom the quality and value of class discussion related to JiTT responses critically depends on students' participation and engagement. Using JiTT, instructors expect that students will complete their pre-class reading in order to apply and discuss new terms and concepts to be included in class that day. To determine whether students changed their level of class preparation as a result of using JiTT, we asked students in an introductory lab-based biology course for majors (Biology K101) three questions to determine whether they were preparing for class:

1. Do you read the web notes before class?
2. Do you do the readings from the text before class?
3. Do you do read the textbook or the class notes (if provided) before class in your other courses?

The results in Table 5.2 show that two-thirds to three-quarters of the students who were scoring in the A, B, or C range after the third exam read the textbook and notes before class, whereas only about half of the same students reported preparing for class in their other course. Students who were not doing

Table 5.2. JiTT Increases Class Preparation

Course grade after taking three exams	Read web notes before class	Read book before class	Read book in other classes
A	78%	67%	55%
B	76%	75%	46%
C	66%	66%	53%
D	48%	42%	44%
F	50%	40%	46%

Students in Biology K101 were asked: Do you read the web notes before class? (Column 2) Do you do the readings from the text before class? (Column 3) Do you do read the textbook or the class notes (if provided) before your other classes? (Column 4) Student responses were grouped according to the course grade they were receiving (A-F) after taking the third of four exams. Number of students: approximately 800.

well in the class—scoring in the D or F range after the third exam of the semester—were also not preparing for class and it is likely that this factor, along with other factors relating to their personal circumstances, was affecting their course performance. Fewer students received grades of D or F in a JiTT class. We have found similar results for an introductory non-major, non-lab course using JiTT (Marrs & Chism, 2005). Although it is difficult to determine the direction of causality between student preparation and course grades, it is clear that the two are positively related. Anecdotally, we believe that JiTT is making a difference. The fact that a higher percentage of students in the A/B/C range report preparing for their JiTT-based course than for other courses suggests that JiTT has a positive effect on student preparation prior to class.

JiTT Improves Student Study Habits

Developing good study habits is one of the most effective ways to succeed in college. Research has shown that students learn more efficiently and retain the information longer when they study regularly; they retain much less information from a single "cram" session (Bybee, 2002; Holloway, 2000; Hoover, 2002; Kirkland, 1979; Bransford et al, 2000). We wanted to determine whether JiTT exercises made a significant difference in student study skills, making it easier for students to study in shorter, more frequent study sessions. Again, we asked students in the introductory lab-based biology course for majors (Biology K101) to report whether they "crammed" for exams in their JiTT-based biology course and other, non-JiTT classes.

As shown in Table 5.3, 48% of A students, 68% of B and C students, and over 70% of D and F students self report that they cram for exams in their non-JiTT classes. However, only 19% of those same A students felt the need to

Table 5.3. JiTT Improves Student Study Skills

Course grade after taking three exams	"Crammed" in Biology K101	"Crammed" in other courses
A	19%	48%
B	36%	67%
C	43%	68%
D	68%	74%
F	66%	71%

Students in Biology K101 were asked to report whether they "crammed" for exams in biology vs. their other, non-JiTT classes. Cramming was defined as "saving virtually all studying for the day or night before or of the exam." Student responses were grouped according to the course grade students were receiving (A-F) after taking the third of four exams. Number of students: approximately 800.

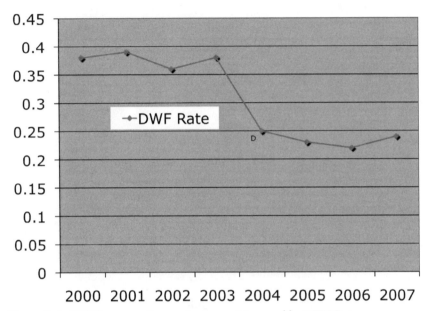

DWF Rate

Figure 5.1. JiTT Improves Course Success as Measured by DFW Rates

We calculated the number of students in Biology K101 who were not successful in passing the class as the number of students who left with a grade of D or F, or who withdrew from the course for any reason (W). The D/F/W rate is shown for Biology K101 for the years indicated. JiTT was introduced in this course in 2004. Similar results are seen for Biology N100 (introductory biology course for nonmajors) as described in the text.

cram for their biology course. Students receiving a B or a C also reported less need to cram in their JiTT-based course (although 36% and 43%, respectively, still felt that they needed to cram). Although a substantial percentage of students who were receiving poor grades in the class still felt the need to cram in a JiTT class, there were fewer students receiving these poor grades in a JiTT class (see Figure 5.1). Again, these results are similar to those we have found in an introductory biology course for non-majors (Marrs & Chism 2005).

JiTT Reduces Course Failure Rates

Introductory courses in biology, as well as some upper level courses that are more conceptual or theoretical in nature (e.g. genetics) commonly exhibit high failure rates (the percentage of students with grades of D, F, or W). Since implementing JiTT in the introductory biology course for non-majors, the D/F/W rate has decreased from 27% to 20%. In the introductory biology course for

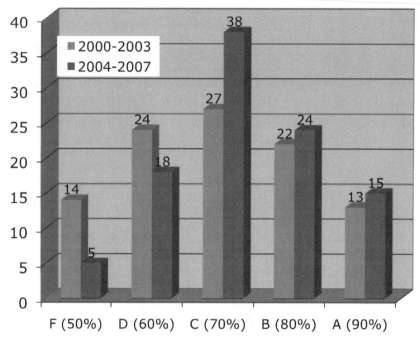

Figure 5.2. JiTT Improves Course Success as Reflected by Grade Distribution

We calculated the number of students in Biology K101 receiving final course grades of A (90% or better), B (80-89%), C (70-79%), D (60-69%), or F (59% or below) in years prior to implementing JiTT in Biology (2000-2003) and after JiTT was implemented in Biology K101 (2004-2007). The percent of students receiving a particular grade is indicated above each bar.

majors (Biology K101) the effect has been even more dramatic, with a reduction in the D/F/W rate from almost 40% to less than 25%, as seen in Figure 5.1. In physics, a similarly significant reduction in course failure rates has been observed with the introduction of JiTT (Gavrin & Novak, 1999). The importance of reducing D/F/W rates in science courses, especially in early "gateway" courses, is particularly important for increasing the number of students who graduate in science, technology, engineering, and math (STEM) fields.

When we look at the grade distribution in the introductory biology course for majors (Biology K101) before and after implementing JiTT, it is apparent that there is a marginal upward shift of grades. As illustrated in Figure 5.2, there are fewer grades of D and F, with a complementary increase in C grades and smaller increases in grades of A and B, suggesting that JiTT has a differentially positive effect on middle-to-lower performing students. Although these data do not control for differences over time in student attributes, the results suggest that JiTT is making a difference in improving student learning outcomes and increasing retention in science-related courses.

JiTT Provides Numerous Opportunities for Students to Receive Formative Assessment

JiTT provides an excellent way for students to receive feedback on their understanding before taking a test for a grade. By treating students' JiTT responses as "works in progress" and providing multiple opportunities for in-class feedback and practice, students are given many opportunities to explore their own thought processes about a particular concept and revise their thinking if necessary. Using three semesters of data, students in the introductory biology course for non-majors report that these multiple opportunities for feedback and reflection are valuable to their learning; 87% of students in this course rated the class discussions of JiTT responses as "very useful to learning the fine points" of a concept (number of responses: 485), while over 94% of students in a single semester (number of responses = 184) reported that the in-class cooperative learning exercises were "highly useful" or "very useful" in promoting understanding of the concepts discussed in class.

JiTT Increases Cognitive Gains in Biology

Using pre/post testing to measure average normalized gains (Hake, 2002) in JiTT and non-JiTT introductory biology courses, we have found a dramatic positive effect from using JiTT, especially when coupled with related in-class cooperative learning exercises. As shown in Table 5.4, students showed the largest average normalized gain (63.6%) on test questions that were reinforced by both JiTT questions and in-class cooperative learning activities. Of the two, JiTT questions seem to have the stronger effect. The average normalized gain with JiTT only was 56%; with cooperative learning only, the normalized gain was 45% (these results are not shown in Table 5.4). Using one or the other teaching strategy led to an average normalized gain of 52%. Students in classes with neither JiTT nor cooperative learning had normalized gains of only 17–21%.

Overall, as the data presented in this section illustrate, JiTT has a strong positive effect on both students' learning and study habits, especially when combined with in-class cooperative learning activities related to the JiTT exercises. JiTT provides numerous opportunities for students to receive formative assessment on their learning progress, primarily through the use of web-based JiTT exercises, increases retention rates in important undergraduate science courses, improves class preparation, reduces "cramming" for tests, and increases cognitive

Table 5.4. JiTT Improves Content Knowledge in Biology

We used the results from a 20-question pre-class and post-class test, calculating the % Gain and Average Normalized Gain as described (Hake 2002, reviewed in Dancy and Beichner 2002).

% Gain (%G):
> (class avg. % correct on post-test)—(class avg. % correct on pre-test)

Average normalized gain <g>:
> % Gain/(100% − class avg. % correct on pre-test)

Teaching Strategies	% Gain	Average Normalized Gain
Questions on tests with *no additional interventions* during semester	Average of 4 questions %G = **15%** (25%–10%)	Average of 4 questions <g> = 15%/90% = **16.7**
Questions on tests *tied to additional back of the book homework problems* during semester	Average of 4 questions %G = **17%** (35%–18%)	Average of 4 questions <g> = 17%/82% = **20.7**
Questions on tests tied to Warm Up (JiTT) *or* cooperative learning questions during semester	Average of 4 questions %G = **45%** (59%–14%)	Average of 4 questions <g> = 45%/86% = **52.3**
Questions on tests tied to Warm Up (JiTT) *and* cooperative learning questions during semester	Average of 4 questions %G = **56%** (68%–12%)	Average of 4 questions <g> = 56%/88% = **63.6**

gains in biology as measured by average normalized gains on exam questions targeted by JiTT exercises, cooperative learning exercises, or both.

CONCLUSION

The experience at IUPUI illustrates that JiTT can successfully be applied in biology courses, resulting in improved student learning. Notably, the outcomes in terms of student self-reported experience, and more importantly in terms of measurable changes in study habits and learning, are similar to results obtained when JiTT was first applied in physics education. The examples of how JiTT has been adopted in biology at IUPUI—as illustrated in this chapter—offer suggestions as to how JiTT might be adapted at other institutions or in other disciplines. In particular, the Arons criteria, originally developed for physics education and applied here in the context of biology, provide a valuable framework for developing effective JiTT questions in a variety of disciplines. Similarly, the combination of JiTT with cooperative learning and *Good Fors* in the biology classroom can readily be adapted in other fields. As the IUPUI results indicate, by promoting pre-class preparation and in-class active learning, JiTT leads not only to increases in student learning, but also to the development of good study habits necessary for student success. More generally, JiTT is consistent with the teaching practices recommended for effective learning listed at the beginning of this chapter, including constructivism, active learning, and use of formative assessment. The result is greater student learning in STEM disciplines and improved student engagement in the learning process.

Notes

1. In addition to JiTT exercises I also use after-class assignments called "What is (Biology) Good For?" that highlight the relevance of biology in everyday life.

2. *Cooperative Learning: Making Connections in General Biology* (Bres & Weisshaar, 2000) is a particularly useful resource for cooperative learning exercises to use in conjunction with the JiTT exercises.

3. "What is———good for?" (substitute a discipline for the blank) activities were part of the original JiTT framework and viewed as important "enrichment materials" to motivate and engage students (see Novak, et al., 1999, p. 25). A sample *Good For* essay, "What is Biology Good For? Keeping Us Healthy During Flu Season: Flu Vaccines," as well as many others, can be found at http://www.biology.iupui.edu/biocourses/N100/archives.html. Note that JiTT exercises ("warmups") and JiTT-informed in-class activities are the primary, and most widely used, components of the JiTT teaching strategy.

References

Alberts, B. M. (2008). Considering science education. *Science, 319*(5870), 1589.

Allen, D., & Tanner, K. (2005). Infusing active learning into the large-enrollment biology class: Seven strategies, from the simple to complex. *CBE Life Science Education. 4*(4), 262–268.

Arons, A. B. (1979). Some thoughts on reasoning capacities implicitly expected of college students. In J. Lochhead & J. Clement (Eds.), *Cognitive process instruction: Research on teaching and learning skills* (pp. 209–215). Philadelphia: Franklin Inst. Press.

Bonner J. J. (2004). Changing strategies in science education. *Science, 306*(5694): 228.

Bransford, J. D., Brown, A. L., & Cocking, R. R. (Eds.). (2000). *How people learn: Brain, mind, experience, and school.* Washington, DC: National Academy Press.

Bybee R., (Ed.). (2002). *Learning science and the science of learning.* Arlington, VA: National Science Teachers Association Press.

Bres, M., & Weisshaar, A. (2000). *Cooperative learning: Making connections in general biology.* Pacific Grove, CA: Brooks/Cole Thompson Learning.

Committee on Undergraduate Science Education (1997). Misconceptions as barriers to understanding science. In Center for Science, Mathematics and Engineering Education, *Science teaching reconsidered: A handbook* (pp. 27–32). Washington, DC: National Academy Press.

Fisher, K. M., Lipson, J. I., Hildebrand, A. C., Miguel, L., Schoenberg, N., & Porter, N. (1986). Student misconceptions and teacher assumptions in college biology. *Journal of College Science Teaching, 15*(4), 276–280.

Gavrin, A. D., & Novak, G. M. (1999). What is physics good for? Motivating students with online materials. *Proceedings of the IASTED International Conference on Computers and Advanced Technology in Education,* 1–5.

Gavrin, A., Marrs, K., Blake, R., & Watt, J. (2000). *The WebScience Project at IUPUI.* Retrieved from site: http://webphysics.iupui.edu/webscience/webscience.html

Hake, R. R. (1998). Interactive-engagement versus traditional methods: A six-thousand-student survey of mechanics test data for introductory physics courses. *American Journal of Physics, 66*(1), 64–74.

Hake, R. R. (2002). Lessons from the physics education reform effort. *Conservation Ecology 5*(2): 28. Retrieved from site: http://www.consecol.org/vol5/iss2/art28/

Handelsman, J., Ebert-May, D., Beichner, R., Bruns, P., Chang, A., DeHaan, R., Gentile, J., Lauffer, S., Stewart, J., Tilghman, S. M., & Wood, W. B. (2004). Scientific teaching. *Science, 304*(5670), 521–522.

Holloway, J. H. (2000). How does the brain learn science? *Educational Leadership, 58*(3), 85–86.

Hoover, J. P. (2002). A dozen ways to raise students' test performance. *Principal, 81*(3), 17–18.

Kirkland, K., & Hollandsworth, J. G., Jr. (1979). Test anxiety, study skills, and academic performance. *Journal of College Student Personnel, 20*(5), 431–35.

Marrs, K. A., Blake, R. E., & Gavrin, A. D. (2003). Use of warm up exercises in just in time teaching: Determining students' prior knowledge and misconceptions in biology, chemistry, and physics. *Journal of College Science Teaching, 33*(1), 42–47.

Marrs, K. A. & Novak, G. M. (2004). Just-in-time teaching in biology: Creating an active learner classroom using the internet. *Cell Biology Education, 3,* 49–61.

Marrs, K. A. & Chism, G. R. (2005). Just-in-time teaching for food science: Creating an active learner classroom. *Journal of Food Science Education, 4*(2), 27–34.

National Research Council (1996). *National Science Education Standards.* Washington, D.C.: National Academy Press .

Novak, G. M., Patterson, E. T., Gavrin, A. D., & Christian, W. (1999). *Just-in-time teaching: Blending active learning with web technology.* Upper Saddle River, NJ: Prentice Hall.

Paulson, D. R. (1999). Active learning and cooperative learning in the organic chemistry lecture class. *Journal of Chemical Education, 76*(8), 1136–1140.

Rutherford, F. J., & Ahlgren, A. (Eds.). (1989). *Project 2061: Science for All Americans.* New York: Oxford University Press.

6

Using Just-in-Time Teaching in the Geosciences

Laura A. Guertin

Just-in-Time Teaching (JiTT) addresses a variety of teaching and learning challenges in college-level introductory geoscience courses (AGU Chapman Conference, 1994). For example, most students enroll in an introductory geoscience course to satisfy a general education requirement and have no plans to take additional courses in this area. Many of these students harbor negative attitudes about science and have minimal interest in the content (Libarkin, 2001). Because lecture is still the primary method of classroom instruction in these courses (Lammers & Murphy, 2002), students have little opportunity to interact with each other or the material in class. As a result, classroom learning remains passive and students feel isolated, adding to the lack of student engagement. JiTT can help break this pattern of disengagement and isolation.

In this chapter I describe how JiTT can be used to help students come to class prepared, engaged, and motivated—and how student responses to JiTT exercises can be used to build greater interactivity in the classroom. In the next section I provide a description of two introductory geoscience JiTT exercises, as well as JiTT-related activities for the beginning and end of a course. In the remainder of the chapter I discuss recommendations for successful JiTT practice, JiTT implementation challenges, and survey results highlighting the impact of JiTT on student learning.[1]

USING JiTT IN TWO GEOSCIENCE COURSES: EXAMPLES

I am the only geologist on my campus, and it does not offer an undergraduate geology degree. Therefore, my role on campus is not to prepare future geologists but to engage students in the content and create a scientifically-literate citizenry. I use the "WarmUp" exercise approach described by Novak, Patterson,

Gavrin, & Christian (1999), except I term my weekly JiTT exercises GeoBytes or DinoBytes, in which students "byte into the latest geoscience news." I assign weekly JiTT exercises that require students to complete three open-ended questions and submit responses prior to the upcoming class via a web-based course management system. The JiTT questions are based on Bloom's taxonomy of cognitive skills (Bloom, 1956). The first question in the JiTT exercise is typically on the lower end of Bloom's scale (knowledge, comprehension, application) and the remaining questions require higher-order cognitive processes such as analysis, synthesis, and evaluation.

The JiTT exercises require student understanding of both lecture content and concepts covered in the reading. Students have mixed views about this, as approximately 60% of my students would rather have the online JiTT questions cover only topics directly related to the lecture than extend beyond the typical course material. Students are given a week (Friday to Friday) to complete each JiTT exercise. The responses are due two hours before class, at which time I review them for use in class. During class I address the learning challenges identified in the student responses, using two to three responses per question to generate classroom discussion. Following discussion of the selected responses I continue with an active learning exercise to reinforce the week's material.[2]

A Detailed Example: The Ethics of Fossil Collecting

The underlying philosophy of JiTT is to engage students by encouraging them to take control of the learning process and become active learners. At the same time I aim to achieve course-related learning goals, in particular building the quantitative and critical thinking skills of non-science majors. To promote student motivation, I must reframe the content and adopt new teaching strategies that encourage students to develop effective problem-solving, collaboration, and communication skills. I have found JiTT to be a valuable way to simultaneously meet all of these learning goals while also obtaining important feedback on the progress of student learning in my courses.

Around mid-semester in my *Dinosaur Extinctions and Other Controversies* course I spend a week on the laws and ethics of fossil collecting, selling, and displaying, a topic not typically addressed in introductory-level geoscience courses. The discussion relating to ethics helps my students become informed and engaged citizens not only with respect to the sciences but also in terms of broader societal issues. Because the course textbook does not address the laws that protect fossils and dictate fossil collecting, all student readings are accessed online, including the National Park Service's description of the Antiquities Act, The Society of Vertebrate Paleontology's description of the Paleontological Resources Preservation Act, articles from National Geographic, and a National Public Radio "Talk of the Nation" audio file on the ethics of fossil hunting and purchasing. The JiTT exercise is posted online on the Friday (afternoon) of the week before we begin the ethics and fossils unit. The online responses are due by 8:30 a.m. on the following Friday, which gives me two hours to review and select student responses to highlight before class. The remainder of this section describes what happens during the week, both in and out of class. This cycle is repeated for each topic throughout the semester.

JiTT Exercise for the Week. The three questions included in the week's JiTT exercise are shown below.

1. If a fossil is found on private land, should a paleontologist be expected to pay the landowner the market value for that fossil before it can be studied? Explain why/why not.
2. Should an amateur collector who originally finds a fossil get co-authorship on a scientific report of the fossil? Or, should the professional paleontologist acknowledge the collector (but not give him or her co-authorship)? Or does the paleontologist deserve sole authorship because of his/her advanced educational background? Explain.
3. Sometimes a paleontologist performs research on certain fossils knowing full well that another researcher is already studying them. What if the first paleontologist scoops the second by submitting the results of their research to a journal for publication first, leaving the second researcher's work to be rejected: "Sorry, that's already been done"? Is this just an example of how science, like other aspects of a capitalistic and goal-oriented society, is a competitive venture? Explain.

Class One: Monday. The week begins with a lecture summarizing the current and proposed laws to protect—sometimes inadequately—fossils such as dinosaur bones. We then discuss potential scenarios related to the topic. For example, if an amateur or professional paleontologist digs up a fossil on public land, does she/he get to keep it? What if the fossil was found on private land? We end the day by exploring online auction sites where fossils are being sold and ask whether it is appropriate to assign a price to a piece of Earth history. A possible question for students to discuss: We cannot sell live human organs online, so why is it acceptable to sell fossilized remains through the Internet? This type of question requires students to share their views, supported by current laws (or the lack of laws).

Class Two: Wednesday. During the second class of the fossil laws and ethics week, we alternate between watching clips of a video, *Curse of T. rex* (NOVA, 1997), and discussing the story of the *Tyrannosaurus rex* named Sue.[4] My students are engaged throughout the class period as the story unfolds, learning not only about fossil collection and property rights laws but also the motivation of each of the people/groups involved in the case (money versus science).

Class Three: Friday, JiTT Review and In-Class Exercise. As soon as the deadline for students' JiTT responses closes I begin reviewing them. The questions require responses that are not found directly in any of the assigned readings. Students must reflect upon the information they have learned from these sources, along with their knowledge of related laws, and apply their own ethical beliefs to this subject, such as who deserves authorship on publications. Such questions allow me to continue to introduce topics and issues relating to laws and ethics with paleontology and research in general, while challenging the students to answer questions that require higher-order thinking based on Bloom's taxonomy.

After discussing representative JiTT responses that highlight lingering issues, students continue to explore the week's theme, "Who owns fossils— physically and scientifically?" by engaging in a small-group exercise focusing on museum curation and collections management.[5] Students are divided into groups of four and are provided with two boxes of miscellaneous whole and broken fossils, some labeled and some not, and a case-based scenario in which a museum has received a fossil collection that must be organized and evaluated as to the cost of storing. In this case the in-class activity extends the concepts and ideas initially raised in the JiTT exercise; in other cases, the in-class activity directly relates to student learning challenges identified in the JiTT responses.

Summary. The JiTT exercise and accompanying in-class activities directly address many of my overarching course goals. I am able to introduce a topic to the students in a way that accommodates a variety of student learning styles and engages students actively in the learning process. Students learn the basic content through a variety of media and then are asked to apply, analyze, and evaluate this information, using their own beliefs to formulate opinions and proposed solutions to issues not unique to paleontology. Students learn the perspective and points-of-view of others during the reporting of JiTT responses. The follow-up in-class activities require students to develop responses to a new situation when presented with partial information. The students also must collaborate with their peers to complete the collections design and quantitative portion of the exercise. Overall, my goal for this course is to help students develop the ability to apply these skills beyond the geosciences. Student comments from the open-ended portion of the JiTT exercise suggest that JiTT is helping to meet these goals.

Using JiTT to Scaffold Student Learning: Another Geoscience Example

The following JiTT exercise was developed for the course, *Earth and Life,* which chronicles the physical and biological changes the Earth has experienced over its 4.6 billion year history. Students first read a unit on marine life from the Paleozoic and Mesozoic Eras and are then asked to think about the anatomic design of fish and reptiles and the transition of life from water to land, using the following cluster of questions in a JiTT exercise:

1. What are the adaptations needed to move from water to land (whether it be an arthropod or a pioneering amphibian)?
2. Could snakes be linked to marine lizards? What are your views and interpretations of the evidence?
3. Let's say I told you that I thought marine mammals evolved independently of land mammals (meaning, both originated on their own in separate environments with no linkages). What evidence would you use to argue that my viewpoint is incorrect, or correct?

A representative student answer for each of these questions is listed below, ranging from a low level to a high level response.

1. Low level response: The adaptations needed to move from water to land are some form of limbs like feet.
2. Medium level response: They are basing the link between the fossils. They have also found anatomical characteristics linking the creature to a group of extinct marine lizards. I think that snakes could be linked to marine lizards because of how marine lizards are. I think snakes started out and marine lizards evolved from the snakes, developing limbs.
3. High level response: I don't think that it's really that crazy of an idea but I do believe that these mammals did evolve from land to water. It is said that in the beginning these animals would live on land but they would go into the water to feed, which could explain some of the changes these animals needed. Scientists compare this change to that

of birds becoming flying animals and humans becoming upright. They have also discovered a whale fossil with hind limbs. These limbs were only 2 feet long and wouldn't have been able to support the creature, so over time these animals lost their need for limbs since they were living in water.

Note that the three questions require increasingly higher levels of cognitive skills to generate acceptable responses. The first question relies on basic knowledge and comprehension, recalling knowledge from lecture and readings. The second question is higher on Bloom's scale as it asks students to analyze and compare. The final question allows students to evaluate information and formulate their own opinions to make a judgment. This scaffolding approach, increasing the difficulty of the questions within the weekly JiTT exercise, helps to create "desirable difficulties" that motivate students to become actively engaged in the learning process. This approach also promotes the development of self-monitoring learners who are able to increasingly transfer their critical thinking skills to new situations.

Using JiTT to Begin and End a Course

The following examples illustrate how JiTT can be used to provide valuable information about students and set the tone for the course (at the beginning of the semester) while also helping students synthesize their learning across the semester (at the end of the semester).

Using JiTT at the Start of the Course. During the first week of classes I use JiTT to learn about students' assumptions and expectations coming into the course and to encourage students to look at the syllabus for the semester. I ask:

1. Why did you decide to sign up for this course?
2. What do you hope to learn in this course? In other words, what knowledge do you hope to get out of this course by the end of the semester?
3. Take a look through the syllabus. What one topic are you looking forward to learning about the most? Why? Are there any topics not on the syllabus you were hoping to learn about? Explain.

These questions allow me to clarify any major misconceptions students have coming into the course. For example, it is typical for students in my *Dinosaur* course to want to focus learning on *Jurassic Park* for the entire semester. These responses provide me the opportunity early on in the course to inform students that we will not be watching movies all semester, and that this geoscience course focuses on science. I also take the opportunity to showcase the best student responses to these questions and explain why these responses are considered complete and would receive a perfect score. Using JiTT in this way helps students better understand the role of JiTT in the course and promotes continuing student motivation to complete the JiTT exercises. It also indicates to students that I take their learning seriously and am willing to invest time (both in and out of class) to respond to their questions and learning challenges.

Using JiTT at the End of the Course. The final JiTT exercise at the end of the semester includes a series of questions that requires students to reflect on course content from the entire semester.

1. In your opinion, what was the most interesting topic you learned about this semester? Why?
2. What is the topic that "shocked and amazed" you the most (meaning, a new piece of knowledge you gained that really surprised you, and not necessarily your favorite topic)? Why?
3. What is the topic you told the most people about (family, friends, co-workers, etc.)? What was their reaction to your information?

These questions provide me valuable feedback that I normally would not receive on end-of-semester course evaluations. Because the questions are graded, students put considerable time and effort into answering these questions. Discussing the responses to these questions during the last class of the semester allows me to conduct a mini-review session before the final exam. The responses also alert me to any changes or clarifications I need to make in the syllabus or to specific exercises in the following semester.

USING JiTT TO PROMOTE STUDENT LEARNING OUTCOMES

JiTT exercises can be adapted to meet a variety of learning goals, all of which promote deep (rather than surface-level) learning and encourage reflective thinking processes. Some of the most important characteristics of JiTT exercises, along with their benefits for student learning, are outlined below.

JiTT promotes student learning. There are many benefits to asking students to provide their own answers on a JiTT question rather than selecting a multiple-choice option on a quiz at the start of class to check their pre-class reading. Although multiple-choice questions are much quicker and easier to grade, open-ended questions challenge students to independently research the answers to questions by integrating material from various sources.

JiTT encourages the participation of all students in the learning process. Because JiTT responses are invisible to other students in the course, all students are able to disclose learning challenges or provide feedback on course content without fear of ridicule by their peers. In particular, students who may be hesitant to speak up in class have the ability to contribute to the discussion anonymously (to other students) by openly sharing their personal viewpoints in their JiTT responses. Only the professor knows the authorship of each response. As one student in my class noted, "I like being able to voice my opinion without having to talk in front of a whole class full of people."

JiTT encourages appreciation for others' perspectives. When JiTT responses are shared in class (anonymously) students see and hear points of view about a subject that differ from their own. In-class follow-up discussion provides an opportunity for students to challenge or support these points of view, with the instructor mediating the discussion, encouraging the use of logical arguments and data to support or refute claims. The following student comment illustrates how this process broadens the learning process, improving learning: "JiTT exercises are helpful because they provide us with a different perspective on things. By discussing our responses in class, it helps to understand the different views on issues."

JiTT helps students apply concepts and make connections. Through open-ended responses to JiTT questions, students are required to apply material from class, their experience, and their own research to a question or problem. Effective JiTT questions provide students with the opportunity to relate course concepts to relevant real-life events or situations. Research from the learning sciences (Bransford, Brown, & Cocking, 2000) indicates that making this type of connection between prior knowledge and new concepts produces learning that is deeper and more durable. As one of my students reports, JiTT is a valuable aid in that process, "helping us relate what we are studying to present day affairs."

JiTT promotes reflective, higher-order thinking processes. Intentionally constructed JiTT questions aimed at higher-order thinking skills require students to think carefully about the material, connect new concepts or ideas to previous knowledge, and reflect on their level of understanding before formulating a response. Such skills not only lead to increased academic success, but also to professional success. Business, industry, and government groups have identified critical thinking and complex problem solving skills as an important type of learning for citizens and workers in the years ahead (Gardiner, 1994). The student comments below are indicative of the way that JiTT exercises promote effective learning habits that improve students' ability to think deeply and critically about course material.

- "At first the DinoBytes felt like 'busy work,' but now I can see that they helped me get more out of the course. If I hadn't been doing DinoBytes, I don't think I would have thought as much about some aspects of the material."
- "They taught me to become a better critical thinker."

IMPLEMENTING JiTT: CHALLENGES FOR INSTRUCTORS AND STUDENTS

Although JiTT pedagogy provides a number of benefits, including promoting higher-order thinking skills, building appreciation for others' views, and encouraging participation of all students in the learning process, JiTT also provides challenges for instructors and students, especially when this pedagogical practice is initially adopted.

Challenges for Instructors

For instructors who have never implemented JiTT, the process often seems overwhelming: developing effective JiTT questions, organizing and selecting JiTT responses to be used in class, adapting classroom discussion and activities based on student responses just before class, grading JiTT responses, and reporting the scores to students. Fortunately, after completing a couple of JiTT exercise cycles most instructors develop a rhythm and flow that makes developing future JiTT exercises easier. In addition, university course management systems greatly streamline the process of posting JiTT questions and submitting, reviewing, and grading JiTT responses. Typically this is done through an online quiz tool that allows instructors to develop open-ended questions, grade responses, provide comments, and record grades in one place.

With respect to grading JiTT exercises, I have found that it is important to assign a point value to the JiTT questions so that students are held responsible for completing the weekly exercises. In the syllabus, I state that I will be looking for complete answers with a complete thought, and that one- or two-sentence responses for each question are not acceptable. I warn students not to plagiarize, and to reference their sources if brief passages from other authors are needed to support their responses. Students are told to put their answers in their own words whenever possible. In each of my courses, I assign fifteen weekly JiTT exercises, each with three graded topic-related questions. A final question, "Below is a space for your thoughts . . . ," is not graded. I score each question on a scale from 0 to 3, using a rubric developed by Kathy Marrs (Marrs, Blake, & Gavrin, 2003; chapter 1, Table 1.3). Students cannot receive credit for a late JiTT submission. Students are informed that there are no make-ups and no excuses allowed for missing the JiTT deadline.

Some instructors are concerned that a weekly "drive-by" type of assignment will not allow for deep learning to take place. My experience suggests that JiTT provides a useful device to promote deliberate, reflective thinking by students rather than the last-minute pre-test cramming that is all too common. In my course I want to engage students in higher-order thinking skills: evaluating and synthesizing information in particular, using geoscience content, concepts, and ideas. A high-priority goal I set for my non-science majors is to develop the capacity to make sense of information that is presented to them, first by reflecting on what they know and what they don't know, then deciding what questions to ask and the ways that they can determine the answers to those questions. The types of questions asked on JiTT exercises, unlike those that appear at the end of chapters in a textbook, can challenge students to think and engage at this deeper level. The key is in developing JiTT questions that address the learning goals that you have developed for your course.

Challenges for Students

Although nearly all students want to achieve academic and professional success, and see value in obtaining a degree, many students come to college with poor study habits. Unfortunately, once set in place those habits are difficult to change. JiTT can help, although it is important to prepare students for what will be to many a new way of teaching and learning. As described earlier, I require students to submit responses to out-of-class JiTT exercises every Friday by 8:30 a.m. Many students are not accustomed to being held accountable for submitting short assignments in a single course every week. I commonly hear that the JiTT exercises are "too much work" for a general education course for non-science majors. Some students have told me that a general education course should not have more than three multiple choice tests during the semester and that additional assignments are "not acceptable," especially when the answers are not readily found in the readings and require additional thinking. I have also been told that it is not fair that I am so strict about the JiTT weekly deadline and will not accept JiTT responses after the submission deadline closes.

Of course, these "concerns" are not unique to a class that uses JiTT. However, they highlight the need to clearly introduce the JiTT process to students at the start of the course and continually remind them of the weekly JiTT postings and submission deadlines throughout the course to avoid negative attitudes about JiTT assignments and participation in follow-up in-class exercises. In addition, providing detailed information in the syllabus about the purpose and process of JiTT exercises goes a long way toward minimizing student resistance.

DOES JiTT WORK? JiTT AND STUDENT (PERCEPTIONS OF) LEARNING

To measure the effectiveness of JiTT in my courses, I distribute end-of-semester surveys asking students to assess the impact of JiTT on their learning and their overall attitudes toward JiTT. Tables 6.1 and 6.2 summarize student responses from spring and fall, 2005 sections of my *Dinosaur Extinctions and Other Controversies* course. The data highlight the positive impact of weekly JiTT exercises on student learning for a majority of the students. Most notably, the data indicate that DinoBytes aided students' understanding of course material, promoted greater student responsibility for learning, and helped students better understand their own learning gaps.

I see my students working weekly through open-ended questions that require higher-order cognitive skills. I see students working together in class, gaining additional practice with quantitative, communication, and group management skills. I see and hear my students using the vocabulary of the discipline as they work through JiTT exercises and discuss JiTT responses in class. I see students connecting ideas across the course and across their lives. Based on my observations, I believe that that students are gaining valuable knowledge and skill development as they complete JiTT exercises—despite what some students may say in their end-of-course surveys.

Table 6.1. Student Perceptions of Learning from DinoBytes, Part I (Spring and Fall Semesters, 2005)

Question	Semester	No help	A little help	Moderate help	Much help	Very much help	Number of Responses
				Percentage of Respondents			
How much did completing DinoByte exercises help your learning?	Spring 2005	10.8	10.8	40.5	35.1	2.7	37
	Fall 2005	4.1	8.2	38.8	34.7	14.3	49
How much did the Friday DinoByte classes help your learning?	Spring 2005	8.1	10.8	27.0	48.6	5.4	37
	Fall 2005	4.1	12.2	26.5	32.7	24.5	49
Allows me to bring in my own ideas and perceptions about the material	Spring 2005	2.8	11.1	33.3	36.1	16.7	36
Allows me to reflect on the material more	Spring 2005	2.9	5.7	25.7	42.9	22.9	36
Helps me to understand the thoughts and perceptions of other students in the class	Spring 2005	14.3	14.3	25.7	34.3	11.4	35

From Guertin et al. (2007). Reprinted with permission

Table 6.2. Student Perceptions of Learning from DinoBytes, Part II (Fall Semester, 2005)

| | Percentage of Respondents | | | | | |
Question	Strongly Disagree	Disagree	Neutral	Agree	Strongly Agree	Number of Responses
Completing the DinoBytes helps me to better understand the course material	3.8	7.5	22.6	39.6	26.4	53
Completing the DinoBytes helps me see what I don't understand about the course material	5.7	7.5	28.3	39.6	18.9	53
Completing DinoBytes makes me feel more responsible for my successes in class	7.7	3.8	19.2	32.7	36.5	52

From Guertin et al. (2007). Reprinted with permission.

CONCLUSION

Even though some students initially balk at the workload JiTT imposes, most strongly support the pedagogy for its impact on their learning. When asked whether the learning gained from JiTT exercises outweighs the effort, nearly 90% of my students responded in the affirmative.[6] Over two-thirds of the students responded that they believe they have learned and remembered more from a course with JiTT exercises compared to courses that did not employ the JiTT technique.

With JiTT, students taking a course outside of their own discipline are encouraged to become active learners, construct new knowledge, voice their opinions, and respect the opinions of their peers. Although these learning outcomes are central to all courses, for students in an introductory non-majors geoscience course they are especially important. As noted on page 101, most students enrolled in these courses are taking them to satisfy a general education requirement and often feel disengaged from the course content, a feeling exacerbated by passive lecture-style teaching common in such courses. As illustrated in this chapter, JiTT is a valuable tool for building student engagement in the learning process, helping to develop the content knowledge and skill set of students to assist them in becoming informed and educated citizens.

Notes

1. For additional information on the use of JiTT in the geosciences, see the Science Education Resource Center (SERC) Starting Point website, **http://serc.carleton.edu/introgeo/justintime/index.html**.

2. The introductory geoscience courses I teach have a maximum of only 30 students in each section. However, JiTT can be adapted for courses with hundreds of students (see Watkins & Mazur, chapter 3, for ideas about how to use JiTT in large-enrollment courses). In addition, JiTT can be implemented in upper-division courses (Linneman & Plake, 2006 and Luo, 2008).

3. Note that some of these questions are related to end-of-chapter discussion questions from Martin's (2006) textbook on the *Introduction to the Study of Dinosaurs*.

4. This 90% complete *T. rex* skeleton was discovered in the Black Hills of South Dakota in 1990. The Black Hills Institute of Geological Research, a group of commercial fossil hunters and preparators, dug Sue out of the ground from the property of a Cheyenne River Reservation ranch. In 1992, the FBI raided the BHI and took possession of Sue until it could be worked out who was the rightful owner to the dinosaur—the commercial paleontologists who found her, the farmer whose land it was dug from, the Cheyenne nation, or the U.S. government. The dinosaur was turned back over to the Native American farmer, who then let Sotheby's in New York auction the

dinosaur for $8.36 million dollars. Sue is currently on display at The Field Museum in Chicago.

5. This exercise is modified from a workshop I participated in with the Paleobiology Training Program at the Smithsonian's National Museum of Natural History.

6. Simkins and Maier (2004, pp. 454–455) report a similar finding.

References

American Geophysical Union Chapman Conference. (1994). *Scrutiny of undergraduate geoscience education: Is the viability of the geosciences in jeopardy?* Washington DC: American Geophysical Union.

Bloom, B. S. (1956). *Taxonomy of educational objectives, handbook I: The cognitive domain.* New York: David McKay Co.

Bransford, J. D., Brown, A. L., & Cocking, R. R. (Eds.). (2000). How people learn: Brain, mind, experience, and school. Washington, D.C.: National Academy Press.

Gardiner, L. F. (1994). *Redesigning higher education: Producing dramatic gains in student learning.* San Francisco: Jossey-Bass.

Guertin, L. A., Zappe, S. E., & Kim, H. (2007). Just-in-time teaching (JiTT) exercises to engage students in an introductory-level dinosaur course. *Journal of Science Education and Technology, 16*(6), 507–514.

Lammers, W. J., & Murphy, J. J. (2002). A profile of teaching techniques used in the university classroom. *Active Learning in Higher Education, 3*(1), 54–67.

Libarkin, J. (2001). Development of an assessment of student conception of the nature of science. *Journal of Geoscience Education, 49*(5), 435–442.

Linneman, S., & Plake, T. (2006). Searching for the difference: A controlled test of just-in-time teaching for large-enrollment introductory geology courses. *Journal of Geoscience Education, 54*(1), 18–24.

Luo, W. (2008). Just-in-time-teaching (JiTT) improves students' performance in classes – Adaptation of JiTT in four geography courses. *Journal of Geoscience Education, 56*(2), 166–171.

Marrs, K. A., Blake, R. E., & Gavrin, D. (2003). Web-based warm up exercises in just-in-time teaching. *Journal of College Science Teaching, 33*(1), 42–47.

Martin, A. (2006). *Introduction to the study of dinosaurs.* Hoboken: Wiley-Blackwell Publishing.

NOVA. (1997). *Curse of T. rex.* WGBH BostonVideo, 60 minutes.

Novak, G. M., Patterson, E. T., Gavrin, A. D., & Christian, W. (1999). *Just-in-Time teaching: Blending active learning with web technology.* Upper Saddle River: Prentice Hall.

Simkins, S. P. & Maier, M. H. (2004). Using just-in-time teaching techniques in the principles of economics course. *Social Science Computer Review,* (4), 444–456.

7

Using Just-in-Time Teaching in the Physical Sciences

Andrew D. Gavrin

I came to IUPUI in the Fall of 1995. That semester I taught a recitation section of Physics 152, the introductory calculus-based mechanics class. I came in full of enthusiasm, with a desire to see my students learn the material and share my excitement about physics. In fact, I accomplished none of this; by the end of the semester I was thoroughly depressed about my teaching ability. Then the student evaluations came and showed that it had been even worse than I thought. Not only had my students "failed to learn," they were deeply offended by my "arrogant" attitude and my efforts to "prove how smart I am." They "could not imagine" how I could be permitted to teach.

Clearly, I had to make big changes. During the next semester, I worked extensively with an IUPUI colleague, Gregor Novak, to develop a new teaching strategy. In large part, JiTT was the outcome of our efforts.[1] For instance, at one point Gregor and I were discussing the question "How can we get students to come to class prepared?" I cannot recall which of us suggested it, but the idea came: "How about putting questions on the web site and make them due before class"? Just-in-Time Teaching (JiTT) was the result (Novak, Patterson, Gavrin, & Christian, 1999). In January of 1996 we posted the first "WarmUp question" (referred to throughout this volume as "JiTT exercises"). Only later did we begin to use student responses to these JiTT questions as the basis for related in-class small-group activities.

One of the most important uses of JiTT is to encourage students to wrestle with conceptually difficult material before they come to class. When it works well students come to class prepared to engage in "minds on" activities focused on new course concepts. Because students are not seeing material for the first time they are better able to apply these concepts and integrate them with their prior knowledge. As a result, student learning is deeper and longer lasting.

It is impossible, in this space, to illustrate all of the uses of JiTT in the physical sciences. The varied assignment types, purposes, levels of instruction, subject areas, student audiences, and instructor preferences comprise a multidimensional space of JiTT possibilities. In the following sections of this chapter, I give a sampling of examples that illustrate the potential scope of JiTT in physics and chemistry: (1) to introduce jargon, (2) to provide practice with estimation, (3) to increase depth of learning, (4) to promote the understanding of visual representations, (5) to connect science to everyday life, and (6) to frame a major topic. In the last section I provide evidence from my courses at IUPUI regarding the benefits of JiTT and discuss its broader implications for student learning. Throughout the chapter I use examples drawn primarily from physics, with a few examples from chemistry. The ideas illustrated by these examples, however, are applicable to a wide variety of disciplines, including those in the humanities and social sciences.

USING JiTT TO PROMOTE LEARNING: SHOWCASING THE POWER OF JiTT

One of the biggest benefits of JiTT is its flexibility. JiTT exercises can be tailored to fit a variety of learning objectives. In this section I introduce a number of ways that JiTT can be used to encourage students to prepare for class and address common learning challenges. The examples are meant to be illustrative; use them to spark your own creativity in adapting JiTT to your courses.

Introducing Jargon

One straightforward use of JiTT exercises is to introduce students to new concepts and technical terms so that they come to class with a basic knowledge of these ideas. This allows the classroom discussion to go into greater depth because time is not spent on tedious activities such as going over definitions. For example, when I introduce the idea of impedance, I ask:

In your own words, please explain what an impedance is.

Students most commonly respond by simply paraphrasing or restating the formal definition given in the text: "It is just the ratio of the current amplitude and the voltage amplitude" or "It is the voltage divided by the current . . ."[2] Other students give a more physical interpretation, such as "It is the total opposition to alternating current" or "It is like resistance in direct current, but includes the reactance of capacitors and inductors." A few students make both statements and many also include an equation.

I use these responses in the classroom, projecting anonymous answers or selections from answers on an overhead to launch a discussion on how physicists characterize and work with alternating current circuits and signals. By projecting the responses anonymously, no one student feels singled out and I make it clear that "making mistakes" is both natural and in fact necessary to learning. This permission to make mistakes, to take a risk in answering questions, is another key feature of JiTT and has a profound effect on both student motivation and classroom participation. JiTT, like any pedagogy that increases interaction between students and faculty, works best when students feel safe in that interaction. JiTT applied with a heavy hand, a sarcastic attitude, or a bored tone is probably no better than a traditional lecture.

For this particular JiTT exercise I often show two examples of student responses that characterize the impedance as a ratio, one of which explicitly refers to amplitude and one that does not. I ask the class whether the difference is important and follow with a brief mini-lecture on why. Later, when I discuss power dissipation I remind the class of this question and ask how impedance and resistance differ, leading to a discussion of power transmission versus dissipation. Ultimately, students have (at least partially) grasped the idea that reactive elements can prevent the transmission of energy even though they do not dissipate energy themselves. Later, when I want to introduce the idea of resonance, I begin by asking if there are circumstances when resistance and impedance are equal.

JiTT exercises can also be used to encourage students to be precise in their use and understanding of technical terms. For example, consider the following:

Please explain in your own words what a focal point is. Try to do this without referring to any particular mirror or lens.

In this case, I have explicitly forbidden the use of examples. I do this for the same reason that I say "in your own words." Specifically, I am trying to head off students who might be tempted to take the easy way out—quoting a definition or textbook example without thinking.

When I first used this question, I naïvely expected students to recognize the technical term and deal with it as such. I was surprised to find that students had many misconceptions about this term that are rooted in common usage. They interpreted "focal point" in the sense of the focal point of a conversation. Common phrases that students use in answering this question are ". . .where the image is focused" or ". . . where the light is most intense." Many students even say something like "...where you are looking." In the class, I combine these with answers that more closely capture the technical meaning, such as ". . . where parallel rays are reflected." The issue I want to emphasize is that the focal point is a property of the lens or mirror, not of the situation.

Providing Practice with Estimation

Another important use of JiTT exercises is to give students practice with estimation skills. In the physics community such problems are called "Fermi Questions," named after Enrico Fermi, who was legendary for his ability to carry out these types of calculations.[3]

In explaining the value of these exercises I point out that the estimation process has great utility in the workplace. For instance, in an engineering setting it is often necessary to determine if a new idea is feasible. A rough, Fermi-type calculation suffices to determine this and is much quicker and easier than a more detailed calculation. I also argue that the process of estimating the "input data" helps develop a sense of the relative scale of different quantities, processes, and effects.

To encourage Fermi-type thinking I use the following activity as part of a JiTT exercise within the first week of the course:

> Let's say you are holding two tennis balls (one in each hand) and let's say these balls each have a charge Q. Estimate the maximum value of Q such that the balls do not repel each other so hard that you can't hold on to them.

The only content knowledge required to answer this question is Coulomb's law, which most students are able to grasp easily. However, in order to answer the question students must also estimate their own strength (the force they can exert) and arm span, and they must do so in SI (International System) units. Only then can they apply Coulomb's law. The key lesson here is not Coulomb's law but the ability to bring experience to bear when information that is needed to do the problem must be estimated.

Some students take to this task readily. They will usually use an example of a known weight they can lift to estimate their strength, then convert from pounds to Newtons. They write responses such as: "A bag of dog food weighs 50 pounds so I'll use 222 Newtons . . ." or ". . . use my own weight, about 700 Newtons." Other students are less clear and take estimation to mean "guess." They often begin this problem with a statement such as "Let's say I can handle 10 Newtons . . ." Still others truly do not understand what needs to be done. They will either skip all physics (". . . say it's about 100 Coulombs"), or opt out ("I don't see how we can do this without being given . . .").

I display a range of answers in class, starting with the "opt outs." Because this JiTT exercise is given early in the semester I explain the purpose of the exercise and assure the students that they will get used to doing this sort of thing. Then I show an answer with values (let's say 1 Newton) and praise this as an example of choosing values to move forward. Finally, I show an "exemplary" answer (I'll use my weight . . .") and praise this further as a way to get a handle on the magnitude of the needed quantity. I stress that this is an excellent approach.

Three additional examples of "Fermi"-type problems are illustrated below, along with possible estimation strategies:

> **Example 1.** You and a close friend stand facing each other. You are as close as you can get without actually touching. If a wire is attached to each of you, you can act as the two conductors in a capacitor. Estimate the capacitance of this "human capacitor."

To complete this problem, a student may approximate the two people as two plates of a parallel plate capacitor. Next, the student may take the two people to be rectangular plates of reasonable dimensions, say 1.0 m², and choose a reasonable distance between the plates, say 1.0 cm. Finally, the student must use the formula for determining the capacitance of a parallel plate capacitor.

> **Example 2.** On a hot day in Indianapolis, it is 97 °F outside and 70 °F inside. Estimate the electrical power needed by an air conditioner that moves 5000 BTU/hr under these conditions.

For this problem the student may assume that the air conditioner has the ideal performance of a Carnot cycle operating between thermal baths at the two temperatures. A student with a more sophisticated understanding will "downgrade" the performance to, say, one half of the ideal value. In my experience most students get the idea but many fail to remember to convert the given temperatures to Kelvin!

> **Example 3.** Suppose you run into a wall at 4.5 meters per second (about 10 mph). Let's say the wall brings you to a complete stop in 0.5 second. Find your deceleration and estimate the force (in Newtons) that the wall exerted on you during the stopping. Compare that force to your weight.

This problem comes early in the first semester course and contains more "coaching" than the previous examples. Students must estimate their own mass to do the problem and identify the correct physics concepts (definition of average acceleration and Newton's second law) but they are not asked to estimate the stopping time or the initial velocity and a solution process is strongly suggested (find deceleration, then estimate the force). A more challenging version of the same problem would simply state, "Estimate the average force you would feel if you ran into a wall."

Increasing Depth of Learning

In the third week of the introductory chemistry course one of the major topics that students must understand is the difference between a physical and a chemical change. To probe this knowledge and encourage deeper thinking, we ask students about a number of processes, for instance:

> *A sidewalk is formed when concrete sets (hardens). Is this an example of a chemical change? A physical change? Explain your choice.*

This question asks students to take their high school understanding to a new level. Most students are familiar with the physical versus chemical change question, but this is a much more complex process than freezing water or burning paper, common examples used in elementary science courses.

Student responses are generally about equally divided, and even those who correctly choose "chemical change" often give answers that indicate a lack of full understanding. Many students who choose "physical change" give reasons that show an analogy to freezing or dehydration, such as ". . . goes from a liquid to a solid" or ". . . it is dried." Others point out that "individual substances are visible" in the final product. Even students who correctly identify the change to be chemical may give answers that do not go to the heart of the matter, such as "water reacts with the other substances . . ." or "A new substance is formed that has different properties." Others identify more classic hallmarks of chemical change such as "Concrete hardening gives off heat," and ". . . is irreversible. You cannot melt it again."

The instructor begins the day's in-class session by discussing excerpts from answers, first taking students through several of the responses that describe the change as physical, emphasizing the aspects of the responses that make sense. Next, the instructor discusses JiTT responses that describe the change as chemical, again emphasizing that the reasoning "makes sense" from a "common sense" point of view. Finally, the instructor points out that both cannot be correct, and asks "Which of these versions is better? That is, which is more accurate from a scientific viewpoint?" In some cases, students are asked to consult with a nearby student before a "vote" is taken.[4] In other cases the instructor will simply highlight the critical points in a more traditional lecture format.

In our advanced thermal physics course we use JiTT exercises that require students to explore the concepts more deeply on their own, as illustrated in the following example:

> *In your travels, you have probably heard that entropy is a measure of "randomness." The book defines entropy to be Boltzmann's constant times the natural log of the number of accessible microstates. Please compare your understanding of "randomness" to your understanding of the formal definition.*

This produces as many answers as there are students in the class. Some students are willing to take on the challenge, describing both their naïve concept of entropy—"to me, randomness means unpredictability . . ." and the formal definition " . . . if there is only one possible state then omega is one and entropy is zero." Others have more difficulty with the formal definition and simply paraphrase it, stating ". . . the more states there are, the more entropy there is." Another group of students either fails to understand the definition or is unable to relate it to the idea of randomness or disorder, as illustrated in the following response: "as omega increases, the 'randomness' increases . . . I must be missing something." Finally, some students pass on my choice of naïve conception and substitute their own. In most cases these students understand entropy as "that which increases" or "that which lowers the efficiency of an engine." Representative responses from this group of students start with: "The way I learned entropy was . . ." and "I understand entropy as being . . ." I use these responses in the classroom to initiate discussion of the statistical definition of entropy. The responses that are most valuable are those in which a student has clearly identified some behavior of the function with a more tangible situation. The reference to a single possible state above is a good example. However, I have not been entirely satisfied with this aspect. Students clearly have read the assignment and have thought about the definition, but I have not found as many responses that I can use in class as I would like.

Promoting the Understanding of Visual Representations

As in many areas of science, students in the introductory chemistry course must learn not only the jargon of the field but also a new "visual language." This language includes many schematic representations of physical objects and processes that can be drawn by hand and that provide a kind of shorthand for representing things that would be difficult or impossible to draw "accurately." To provide students with practice in this representational skill, the following JiTT question is asked in conjunction with Figure 7.1:

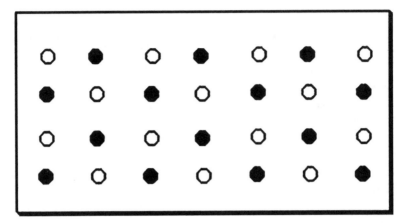

Figure 7.1.

The picture below depicts matter at the submicroscopic level. Describe what you see and take a guess as to what the identity of the substance is.

What is extraordinary about this question is the large number of students who focus not on the orderly arrangement of the "atoms" or on the fact that there are clearly two "kinds," but on their size and spacing. They give answers that include phrases such as "The atoms are widely spaced . . ." and "In a liquid, the atoms would be closer together . . ." A large number of students conclude that the substance is a gas based on this reasoning.

In the classroom the instructor contrasts these types of answers with those that focus on other aspects of the drawing. Students learn not only to identify materials by the degree and type of order exhibited, but they also gain an appreciation for how difficult it would be to draw a solid in an "accurate" way. This topic can be referred to throughout the semester as new ways of schematically illustrating chemical bonds, charges, and other phenomena are introduced.

Connecting Science to Everyday Life

JiTT questions are well suited to helping students connect relevant, real-life experiences with classroom concepts. To illustrate, consider the following JiTT exercise used in an introductory chemistry course:

John has suddenly become very concerned with his weight. He weighed the amount of food and drink ingested and learned that he consumes 3 pounds of food and drink a day. He weighed his stools, urine and sweat and found that he only excretes 2.2 pounds of "stuff" a day. How fast is John gaining weight? What might be wrong with his analysis?

This is a wonderful example of a JiTT question that both connects the classroom science to everyday life (rather more explicitly than some might like) and also asks students to explore a new idea before it is introduced in class. It is used to introduce the idea of balancing chemical equations. It is not direct, in the sense that no chemical equation is mentioned in the question, but gives students practice with the process of balancing inputs (reactants) and outputs (products).

Another example, also drawn from an introductory chemistry course, uses a real-life scenario to give students practice with unit conversions:

> *A professor overheard a bar conversation between two Texans (true story). One claimed that the 1990 Formula 350 Firebird had a bigger engine than the 1995 5.7 L Trans Am Firebird because "back then" they didn't have to worry about fuel economy. The other argued that Pontiac increased the size from 350 cubic inches to 5.7 L in response to high sales of the 5.0 L Ford Mustang. Who is right? Do a calculation before you answer and bring your calculation to class.*

This question is used at the start of the semester to introduce the idea of unit conversions and to accustom students to using a known unit conversion (most can convert centimeters to inches) to determine a more complex one (converting from cubic inches to liters). The instructor discusses the (many) common mistakes and then presents a mini-lecture describing how the conversion should be done.[5]

Framing a Major Topic

In the JiTT example below students are asked to wrestle with the first law of thermodynamics—but this is not explicitly stated in the question. Instead, students are left to make this connection on their own:

> *Is it possible to add heat to an ideal gas without changing its temperature? If it is possible, please explain how it is done.*

This question inevitably produces a wide range of answers. A significant number of the student responses reveal a significant misconception that heat can be "dissipated" at the molecular level. Students often answer the question in the affirmative, stating that "It can be done . . ." and add that "It must be done slowly enough for the atoms to dissipate heat," or "This is an isothermal process, and must be slow enough for the temperature to be maintained." Other responses illustrate a different misconception that leads to the same result, but displays a much less serious misunderstanding of physics. Students in this group know that the temperature can be held constant as long as the heat is causing a phase transition, answering for example: "... can be done at a phase transition." It is true that a real substance can maintain constant temperature while heat is added at a phase transition, but the definition of an ideal gas precludes this possibility.

Some students indicate that it is possible, using the equation-based argument, "because PV = nRT, you can increase the V" or "PV = nRT so pressure and volume must be changed to keep T constant." Exemplary answers either quote the first law of thermodynamics or simply indicate that work needs to be done in equal measure to the added heat, concluding, for example "... if we allow the heat to be used to do work" or "... the gas is doing work that is equal to the heat." Other students will indicate that it cannot be done; they will identify the direct correspondence between temperature and internal energy for an ideal gas. A typical phrase is: "...because the internal energy of an ideal gas depends only on its temperature".

In class I first deal with the "dissipation misconception" noted above, providing a brief overview of atomic collisions. Similarly, I remind students that "ideal" means that there are no interactions between the molecules of the gas, so a phase transition cannot occur.

Next, I indicate that several students correctly stated the relationship between temperature and energy and agree that if no other energy is allowed in or out of the gas, then adding heat must cause a temperature increase. I conclude with the question: "But what if some other form of energy transfer occurs?" This leads me to discuss answers that implicitly invoke the First Law, such as: "the gas is doing work that is equal to the heat." From this, I develop the First Law in the form $\Delta U = Q - W$. Finally, I conclude with an answer that includes the First Law explicitly.

DOES JiTT MATTER?

Once frequent communication has been established among faculty and students, many new windows of opportunity open. The example below illustrates this potential. I had been using JiTT for many years before I began to do this. Since the purpose of the JiTT exercise was to prepare for class, I had always struggled with what to do when the class was to be used as a review session prior to an exam. I tried creating "review JiTTs" but these were never successful. I often simply had a "no JiTT day." A few years ago, though, I began using this as an opportunity to get a quick snapshot of student attitudes. Table 7.1 represents a single JiTT assignment, used as a "minisurvey."

This "assignment" takes only a few minutes for students to complete and provides the instructor with a quick insight into how students perceive the value of JiTT. I have used similar instruments to assess students' attitudes towards other class components. Other instructors may find it valuable to use such a tool to assess office hours, a tutoring center, lecture demonstrations, etc. The results shown represent student responses from two semesters combined. A total of 66 students answered the multiple choice questions. Twenty of those gave some written comments, many quite detailed. As indicated in the multiple choice portion, most students' reactions to the JiTT exercises were quite positive. Common responses included " . . . they force me to open the book and learn . . ." and " . . .they are a pain, but they help me prepare . . ." The negative comments mostly focus on the amount of time students spend on the assignment, e.g., " . . . they are time consuming" and " . . .take too much time." Some students will go on to say "I spend more time on physics than other classes . . ."

Whatever else JiTT has done, it has surely improved me as a teacher. I can see this in my students' achievements and in their desire to take more physics courses after my class is over. My students see it this way, too. They have said

Table 7.1. Responses to End-of-Course Student Surveys

Survey Question	Percentage of students responding "Yes"
Do the JiTT exercises help you to be well prepared for lecture?	80.3%
Do any of your other classes have better ways to help get prepared?	12.1%
Do you feel that the JiTT exercises help you to stay focused in lecture?	57.6%
Do any of your other classes have better ways to help you stay focused?	18.2%
Do the JiTT exercises help you to feel like an active participant in the classroom?	59.1%
Do any of your other classes have better ways to help you be an active participant?	18.2%
Do you feel that the JiTT exercises help make the classroom time useful?	72.7%
Do any of your other classes have better ways to improve the use of the class time?	21.2%

in surveys, focus group interviews, letters to administrators, and other formal and informal ways that they "like" JiTT. They do not say that they "like" me, or that it makes the class easy. They say that they are learning, that they are staying caught up, that they understand what is expected of them, and that they understand how physics fits in with their lives and their educations. This is the most rewarding aspect of the entire JiTT enterprise.

Notes

1. This material is based on work supported by the National Science Foundation under Grant No. DUE-9981111. Any opinions, findings, and conclusions or recommendations expressed in this material are those of the author(s) and do not necessarily reflect the views of the National Science Foundation. I would also like to thank my colleagues in chemistry, Dr. Robert Blake and Mr. Keith Anliker, who created the chemistry examples I have cited here.

2. The responses used throughout this chapter describe categories of representative student work rather than verbatim responses.

3. Probably the most famous Fermi question (attributed to Fermi himself) is "Estimate the number of barbers in Chicago." The business of Fermi questions is now so deeply ingrained in physics that the Science Olympiad includes a "Fermi Questions Competition" in which students work in pairs to complete 30 such questions in 50 minutes.

4. This could be done using personal response systems (clickers), color-coded cards, or simply by raising hands. Watkins & Mazur (chapter 3) provide extensive information on the in-class use of clickers and peer instruction in conjunction with JiTT.

5. For those of you trying out this JiTT question yourself, 5.7 liters is approximately 350 cubic inches.

References

Novak, G. M., Patterson, E. T., Gavrin, A. D., & Christian, W. (1999). *Just-in-time teaching: Blending active learning with web technology.* Upper Saddle River, NJ: Prentice Hall.

8

Using Just-in-Time Teaching in Economics

Mark H. Maier and Scott P. Simkins

As described by Gregor Novak and Evelyn Patterson in the opening chapter of this book, Just-in-Time Teaching (JiTT) was initially developed in the mid-1990s to promote student learning in physics. Intrigued by the success of this pedagogical innovation in promoting active, engaged learning, we initiated a National Science Foundation project in 2000 adapting JiTT pedagogy for economics instruction with the aim of providing economists with a pedagogic alternative to the traditional lecture method, the dominant teaching strategy in the discipline.[1] More broadly, we were interested in determining whether pedagogical innovations developed in one discipline (physics) could be successfully adapted in another discipline (economics).

Although our formal research project had broad goals, our initial motivation for investigating JiTT's benefits was narrower and more personal. Like Novak and Patterson, we were growing increasingly frustrated with students who showed up day after day unprepared for our classes, passively waiting for us to provide the information they needed to successfully navigate the course. As a result we began searching for ways to increase student motivation and active engagement in the learning process—or at least get students prepared for class each day. Early on we recognized that JiTT exercises—activities that require students to submit responses to questions on material to be covered in the next class just a few hours before that class—provided a powerful incentive for students to read before class. As we became more experienced with JiTT, however, we learned that it had much more to offer. It turned out that we, as instructors, also were unprepared for class because we were unaware of what our students brought to the classroom. What did our students know already? What were their prior experiences with the course content? What sections of the reading were already mastered, and which sections remained problematic?

In the end, the biggest benefit of implementing JiTT in our courses was not in having students come to class prepared. Rather, JiTT helped us to better design what went on in class to more effectively address the learning challenges of our students that were made visible in their JiTT responses. In addition, we learned to use JiTT exercises as a way to more actively engage students in class, thereby increasing students' motivation to complete the out-of-class JiTT exercises. In other words, JiTT exercises became more than just another assignment; JiTT helped us redesign what occurred before class and what occurred in class in a way that directly addressed concepts and ideas that students were having difficulty with. Overall, our formal classroom testing (Simkins & Maier, 2004) indicated that JiTT had a modest, positive, statistically-significant effect on students' learning. For us personally, JiTT had a profound effect on the way that we view student learning, how we approach our teaching, and how our classes are conducted.

In the remainder of this chapter we first describe ways that Just-in-Time Teaching helps students learn better and economics instructors teach better, and then discuss how JiTT exercises—the core of the JiTT pedagogy—can be written most effectively in economics and how student responses to these exercises can be used in class to foster active and collaborative learning. We end with a brief discussion of JiTT's effectiveness in promoting student learning in economics based on the empirical evidence that we have collected in our own principles-level courses.

HOW JUST-IN-TIME TEACHING HELPS STUDENTS LEARN

In our economics courses we use JiTT exercises in much the same way that other authors in this volume have described: students respond to a small group of questions focusing on material that will be covered in the next class and submit their responses a few hours prior to class using course management tools such as Blackboard or Moodle. Once submitted, we review students' JiTT responses and use them to organize and inform the upcoming classroom session. Selected student responses—which typically highlight common mistakes, misconceptions, or inconsistencies—are projected (with identifying names removed) at the start of class and are used to direct classroom discussion and develop related in-class cooperative learning exercises.

We have been amazed at how the use of student responses to initiate whole-class or small-group discussions at the start of class transforms the classroom learning environment. Rather than rewarding passive information gathering,

JiTT makes students collaborators in the learning process. Students respond by actively engaging in the discussion of their work! It is not surprising that JiTT helps students become more engaged in the learning process, and as a result, helps them learn more effectively.

To begin with, JiTT techniques are consistent with research on effective teaching and learning, including Chickering & Gamson's (1987) *Seven Principles for Good Practice in Undergraduate Education,* a widely referenced list of "best practices" for college teaching distilled from decades of research on undergraduate education. According to Chickering & Gamson, good practice in undergraduate education:

- encourages contact between students and faculty.
- develops cooperation among students.
- encourages active learning.
- gives prompt feedback.
- emphasizes time on task.
- communicates high expectations.
- respects diverse talents and ways of learning.

As noted in Simkins and Maier (2004, p. 446), "JiTT pedagogy effectively supports each of (these) educational principles and provides the basis for creating a stimulating learning environment that enhances student learning." Simkins and Maier (2004, p. 447) further summarized the practical benefits of using JiTT to carry out these principles in practice: "(1) students are more likely to be prepared for class, (2) use of students' JiTT responses in class creates a positive feedback loop that promotes further learning, and (3) instructors are more aware of student thinking processes."

Just-in-Time Teaching is also well suited for addressing critical student learning issues highlighted in *How People Learn* (Bransford, Brown, & Cocking, 2000), a seminal publication summarizing thirty years of learning science research. According to *How People Learn,* instructors can improve student learning by intentionally focusing their teaching efforts on the following issues:

- **Understanding students' prior knowledge.** Students don't come into our classes as blank slates—their prior knowledge affects what they learn—and what they learn is often different from what we're teaching.
- **Developing expert (vs. novice) performance and learning.** Experts use structured mental models to order and categorize new information; novices tend to focus on surface properties and often fail to develop the structured mental models that characterize expert learning.

- **Promoting transfer of learning.** For students to develop the ability to transfer knowledge to new situations they must be given the opportunity to apply new knowledge in a variety of situations and contexts.
- **Providing frequent formative assessment.** Assessment is critical to provide students with feedback on their learning; assessment should include both content knowledge and process knowledge (e.g. how students solve problems).
- **Helping students become reflective learners (metacognition).** We help students become self-directed learners by encouraging student reflection about the learning process and how learning is being achieved.

As in the case of Chickering & Gamson's (1987) *Seven Principles,* well-crafted JiTT exercises and follow-up in-class activities can address each of these areas. What is required is an intentional focus on developing JiTT questions and activities that address not only the content, concepts, and ideas of the discipline but also the process of learning them. For example, whenever possible we design JiTT exercises that ask students to connect new economic concepts to previous experience or conceptual understandings, and encourage students to not only provide a correct answer, but also to describe how they arrived at that answer. The examples included in this chapter provide additional insight on how to best incorporate these ideas into JiTT exercises.

In addition to being consistent with research on effective teaching practices and how students learn, JiTT also addresses challenges specific to the learning of economics. The economics-related examples below illustrate how JiTT exercises address both issues.

- **Economics course content often is not what a student expected.** For example, when starting a chapter on financial markets in a principles-level course, students will often expect to learn stock picking tips. Instead, they are presented with economic theory explaining why stock-picking may not work. JiTT exercises help prepare students for topics that will be taken up in the upcoming class. Such preparation can decrease the dissonance that would otherwise occur in class when the concepts presented are not what the students expected.
- **Terms are used in technical ways in economics that differ from everyday usage.** Students are less likely to be misled when they are aware that a term will be used differently in class than it is in their everyday lives. For example, students in introductory macroeconomics courses often fail to grasp economists' meaning of the term "investment," which focuses on the

purchase and implementation of capital goods such as machines and computers in production. Instead, students typically continue to rely on their everyday understanding of "investment" as the purchase of equities, even after studying macroeconomists' formal use of the term. This misunderstanding has implications for additional knowledge building, often leading to conceptual difficulties in explaining theories of economic growth or using those theories for policy analysis.

- **Everyday experience may or may not be relevant in economics.** The initial reaction of learners new to a field is to attempt to apply the concepts they are learning to their own lives. In many cases these "common sense" connections are useful for building on previously learned knowledge. However, such immediate application is not always possible and thus may cause a student to prematurely reject the concept. Pre-reading can prepare students to better understand how a concept will be used—for example, in economic modeling that may involve initial assumptions that make it difficult to apply a concept immediately to personal experience. Other concepts may differ in their application on the individual versus the social level because of the fallacy of composition. In both cases, JiTT exercises can help students understand when it is appropriate to apply economic concepts to individual experience.

- **Diagrammatic techniques used in economics require repeated practice in varying contexts.** In order for an analytical device to become an effective part of a student's problem-solving tool-kit, it needs to be used in varying contexts, preferably presenting "desirable difficulties" that positively extend students' intellectual abilities. In many cases the analytical and graphical tools taught by economists become mechanistic devices that generate correct answers only in limited situations and without student understanding of their conceptual power (and limitations). For example, a supply and demand diagram looks deceptively simple but actually contains sophisticated assumptions about *ceteris paribus,* dynamics, boundaries of the market, and abstractions about the market maker. Only by having the opportunity to practice new knowledge in multiple settings will students begin to move beyond the mechanical application of simple economic tools to more critical usage of these tools. Just-in-Time Teaching exercises can both identify novice-level thinking patterns and give students the practice they need to move toward more expert-like thinking in economics.

HOW DOES JUST-IN-TIME TEACHING
BENEFIT INSTRUCTORS?

As illustrated above, JiTT pedagogy, when used intentionally to promote student learning, addresses issues highlighted in learning sciences research and satisfies the principles of good teaching practice. For instructors, one of the biggest benefits of the JiTT approach is that it generates insights on student thinking that otherwise would remain private, and therefore unavailable to benefit both the instructor and the students.

On a very practical level, students' responses to JiTT exercises frequently provide us with examples or insights relevant to the students' lives, which are often different from our experience as instructors from a different generation. The impact on student motivation of using their examples in class is difficult to measure but easy to see. In addition, student responses to JiTT questions sometimes reveal unexpected student knowledge about the economy—such as the use of new technology or experiences with foreign economies—that is different from ours and can be used to enrich classroom discussion.

More often, however, student JiTT responses reveal unexpected gaps in fundamental understanding of economic concepts (such as marginal vs. sunk costs), institutions (role of government in determining prices), policies and policymakers (fiscal vs. monetary policy), basic mathematical measurements and concepts (millions vs. billions and slope/derivatives) or relative magnitudes of economic statistics (population of the U.S., the relative size of federal spending and its components). Often these gaps remain hidden to instructors until after exams, quizzes, or homework assignments are graded, by which time the instructor and students have typically moved on to the next course topic.

Most importantly, JiTT pedagogy enables instructors to better understand student preconceptions as they enter the classroom. Long-time economics instructors know through experience what concepts tend to be most troublesome for principles-level students, whether marginal benefit-marginal cost analysis, elasticity, or economic growth, but we seldom know why these concepts are consistently problematic. With JiTT, we have the potential to better understand students' thinking processes so that we can better spend time in class addressing the underlying causes of the difficulty. Every semester we learn new things from students' JiTT responses about the ways that students think about economic concepts; knowledge that we can use to make our teaching more efficient and more effective. For example, through our analysis of JiTT question responses we know what concepts are well understood and therefore can be treated quickly in class, and what concepts are creating difficulties for students and need classroom reinforcement through hands-on cooperative learning activities. In addition, we can identify misconceptions that are especially strong or unique and that are likely to get in the way of student learning. For example, students may fall into the fallacy of composition, reducing all behavior to individual actions, or may misunderstand "marginal" thinking or the difference between price levels and inflation rates. All of these limit student success in economics but often remain unidentified until after students receive poor grades on an exam or assignment. JiTT exercises help to address these misconceptions in a systematic way with little penalty and while the concepts are still fresh in students' minds.

Overall, our experience has been that by making student thinking processes visible to the instructor, JiTT pedagogy fundamentally changes the way we teach. Initially, JiTT may seem like just another way to have students practice economic concepts or to ensure that students come to class prepared. To be sure, JiTT helps to promote better student learning in exactly these ways, but we think that the most profound effect comes in changing the way that instructors think about their own teaching, and more important, the learning of their students. JiTT exercises help to make instructors more aware of the learning challenges facing their students and the underlying causes for those challenges. Once understood in this way, instructors using JiTT pedagogy adapt their use of classroom time in response to students' responses to JiTT exercises, which has the added benefit of increasing student motivation for completing the JiTT exercises in the first place. The result is greater student motivation and engagement, and more learning.

SUGGESTIONS FOR USING JUST-IN-TIME TEACHING

As we (and authors of other chapters in this book) have noted, Just-in-Time Teaching has the potential to significantly improve student learning in a variety of disciplines. Yet, like any pedagogical innovation, how Just-in-Time Teaching is actually used by instructors greatly affects how successful it will be in improving student learning outcomes. Below we offer a "bakers' dozen" of suggestions based on our own experience on how to increase the success of JiTT pedagogy in your own classes.

- **Let students know that you will be using JiTT in the course, why you are using it, and how it works.** Explain to students the benefits of JiTT and how it will be used so that it is not perceived as an "add-on" in the class but rather as an integral and intentional framework for improving learning and succeeding in the course. Include a discussion of the benefits of JiTT in your syllabus and information about the role of JiTT exercises in the course grade, along with a rubric on how their individual responses will be assessed.

- **Use JiTT regularly . . . but not too often.** In our experience, one JiTT exercise per week is about right, which will result in twelve to fifteen JiTT exercises during a semester. Assigning more than this leads to "JiTT fatigue," especially when used in addition to traditional homework assignments, papers, and other activities.

- **Make JiTT exercises count toward the final grade.** We typically assign ten percent of the total grade to JiTT exercises, sufficient to motivate students to complete the exercises, yet small enough so that JiTTs are perceived as a formative first step toward more important assessment that will come later in the course. In our experience, this percentage of the course grade is enough to result in an 80–85% completion rate for each JiTT exercise in a principles-level course.

- **Include a "what is still unclear" question as part of your JiTT exercise.** To promote metacognition and to gain valuable feedback about your students' understanding of the material, include a question of the type, "After completing this assignment, what is still unclear to you?" The responses will help you target in-class instruction and provide additional ideas for cooperative learning activities that address the identified conceptual difficulties.

- **Write JiTT questions with learning sciences research in mind.** Keep in mind the lessons from learning sciences research on developing expert knowledge, uncovering misconceptions, promoting transfer of knowledge, and building students' metacognitive skills and use them to intentionally develop JiTT questions that address conceptual understanding and thinking processes, not just course content.

- **Look for patterns in students' responses to JiTT questions.** When analyzing students' JiTT responses it is typical to find three or four types of common errors in student thinking about a concept. Group these responses and select one representative response from each group to show at the beginning of the next class. Use these responses to inform the development of in-class cooperative learning exercises that address the identified misconceptions or reasoning flaws.

- **Link students' responses to JiTT questions to in-class exercises.** JiTT is most effective when both students and instructors view it as integral to the course. That means using the knowledge gained from students' responses to intentionally develop collaborative, hands-on activities that provide additional practice and intentionally address learning gaps identified in the students' responses. Doing this reinforces for students the importance of completing the JiTT exercises and the understanding that they are co-collaborators in the learning process—and what they say, even when it is initially flawed or incomplete, matters for what happens in the course.

- **Use JiTT questions on exams and use students' responses as distractors in multiple-choice questions.** Again, this reinforces the idea that the JiTT exercises matter and provides an opportunity for students to show that they have learned from their previous mistakes. Using multiple-choice distractors drawn from students' JiTT responses helps to determine which students are accurately learning the course concepts and provides empirical evidence of areas for future teaching improvement.

- **Keep JiTT exercises short and manageable.** JiTT questions should require students to think carefully about course readings (not simply find a correct answer) but should be written so that they can be answered in a paragraph or two. This requires instructors to apply the Goldilocks principle to JiTT question development—not too easy, not too hard, but just right. Remember, the focus is on getting students prepared for class and identifying gaps in learning prior to addressing this material in class—and note that you've got to read and mentally process these responses relatively quickly in preparation for the next class a few hours after they are turned in, often a useful way to bring practical focus to potential JiTT questions. Keeping this idea in mind, it is possible to use JiTT even in large enrollment classes.

- **Ask students how they reached their answer.** Doing this helps to build students' metacognitive skills and provides valuable information on student thinking processes. Understanding why students are getting problems or concepts wrong is critically important to helping them overcome their learning difficulty. JiTT exercises can help to make this visible to both the student and the instructor.

- **Make JiTT responses easy to submit and manage.** Course management systems such as Blackboard or Moodle facilitate submission of JiTT exercises and instructor record-keeping and make it easy to comment individually to students about their JiTT responses.

- **Grade student responses to JiTT exercises based on evidence for engagement with the reading, not correct answers.** JiTT exercises are meant to be largely formative in nature. Students are not expected to have mastered all of the conceptual material covered in a JiTT exercise. As a result, students should be graded more on the effort involved in answering the question than on the complete "correctness" of the answer. Kathy Marrs (chapter 1, Table 1.3) has developed a useful rubric for grading JiTT responses that is both easy to understand and transparent to students.

- **Provide personal feedback if possible.** Although this varies in practice, whenever possible it is useful to give students short written feedback on their JiTT responses in addition to a numerical score. This personal feedback increases student motivation and builds important connections between students and the instructor.

WRITING EFFECTIVE JiTT QUESTIONS IN ECONOMICS: A COLLECTION OF EXAMPLES

In our experience, JiTT exercises—a set of one or more questions focused on a particular course topic or concept that will be addressed in the upcoming class—are most effective when connected to important learning outcomes for the course. That is, they should not be extraneous assignments perceived by students as add-ons to the core course activities and assessments, but rather should be integrated into the overall structure of the course in an intentional manner. It is also important to keep in mind that JiTT exercises need not ask students to perform tasks that demonstrate the final learning outcomes, but more likely involve skills, observations, or reflections that are steps leading up to these more ultimate goals. That is, JiTT exercises should be viewed as devices for "scaffolding" the learning of students.

Consider, for example, the following JiTT question we use when teaching the concept of present discounted value in a principles-level course:

> You and your brother have inherited a US government bond that will pay $10,000 in ten years but will not pay any interest before then. You agree to share the bond equally, but your brother would like to receive his share of the bond's value now. How will you explain to your brother, who has not studied economics, how much you should pay him for his share?

Note that this JiTT question does not ask students to perform a present discounted value calculation, nor does it ask directly about the concept, or even include all the information needed to use it (in particular, the discount rate is omitted). Instead, students are asked to identify the situation as one requiring present discounted value and to explain to someone with a similar novice background (essentially explaining to themselves) how the concept will be used. This type of question builds not only conceptual understanding but also metacognition, a key step in developing deep and durable learning. As we noted earlier in this chapter, using JiTT questions to intentionally target both content knowledge and conceptual understanding using the research results of the learning sciences increases the chances that JiTT exercises will have the intended effect of improving student learning.

We find it useful to have a varied toolkit of JiTT questions at our disposal. In this way we can vary the task that any specific JiTT exercise requires so that these excercises don't become repetitive throughout the semester. At the same time, we often repeat a format so that students can practice a particular skill, responding to our comments after its first use. Listed below are several types of JiTT exercises that we have found applicable in economics, including one or more examples for each type.[2]

- **Apply a concept to your own life: make an analogy.** This makes explicit a tool that economics instructors, relative experts in the field, regularly use in class to make abstract economic ideas more relevant for students. These types of questions help students build important metacognitive skills and are particularly valuable when course concepts are abstract and students may need assistance in seeing connections to their own experiences.

    Example: The textbook defines automatic stabilizers and discretionary fiscal policy. Give an example from your own experience that provides a similar distinction between "automatic" and "discretionary." Please use an example that is *not* based on macroeconomics, but is based on your experience at home, with your hobby, at work, or at school.

    Example: The supply and demand analysis presented in the textbook looks carefully at the impact of prices on quantity demanded and quantity supplied. Other variables such as income are called "determinants." They are held constant in order to look first at the effect of price changes. In your own life, you often think about things by considering one most important variable while holding the others constant for the time being. Describe one of these situations, clearly describing: 1) what you are investigating (it could be something from your academic interest, your hobby, your work life, or your home life). What is it that you want to know? 2) what single variable you will allow to change. 3) what other variables you will hold constant in order to focus on the impact of the single variable that changes.

Example: Develop a verbal model to explain the relationship between two variables that describe the behavior of an activity related to your own personal experience (e.g. time spent studying and your grade on the upcoming exam). Also, how would you illustrate your model graphically? What would the graph look like? Explain.

- **Interview someone.** This is useful when students need practice applying a concept in different contexts.

  Example: Using the concepts from the assigned reading in your textbook, interview someone about his or her "demand for money." Do not identify the person by name. Specify how much and in what form this person has a "demand for money."

- **Consider multiple perspectives on complex policy decisions.** These types of questions are helpful when students need assistance understanding the logical argument behind competing positions, including those with which they disagree. An interesting macroeconomic question that is always relevant relates to competing political views on economic policy. An alternative question may simply ask students to consider the economic impact of competing economic policy options.

  Example: What are today's fiscal policy options? Often the major U.S. political parties disagree about the appropriate fiscal policy. The following questions are grounded in this issue. Find Republican Party and Democratic Party views on the role of fiscal policy options in their respective party platforms. (Use www.google.com to search for the "Republican Party Platform" and the "Democratic Party Platform.") In what ways do the views differ? In what ways are they similar?

  Example: During a period of stagflation, what policy decision should the Federal Reserve make: raise or lower interest rates? What economic arguments can you make to support your decision?

- **Analyze public use of economic concepts.** Related to the previous example, politicians sometimes use economic concepts correctly—and sometimes they don't. The following example asks students to make this distinction, helping them solidify their own understanding of economic ideas.

  Example: Find at least one argument by each political party that uses an economic concept that we have studied in the course. Is the concept used correctly? How do you know?

- **Analyze/Comment on a Political Cartoon.** Analyzing the economic content of economics-related political cartoons is a good way to promote students' understanding of economic concepts. Political cartoons are sufficiently abstract that they require students to fill in the details of the economic concepts, yet are relevant enough to provide sufficient motivation for students.

  Example: One favorite cartoon that we have used for assignments and exams contains two nearly identical frames, one showing an economist yelling out "SAVE!" and the other showing a similar-looking economist yelling out "SPEND!" This cartoon is perfect for getting students to distinguish the short-run from the long-run implications of their actions. We usually accompany the cartoon with the following questions: How can economists be advocating consumers to both "save" and to "spend" at the same time? Isn't this a contradiction? Explain.

  You can access libraries of economics-related political cartoons online at sites such as slate.com's "Today's Cartoons" http://cartoonbox.slate.com/static/17.html and "Today's Best Cartoons" http://www.cagle.com/politicalcartoons/ or through a google.com search.

- **Analyze an editorial or news story.** Similar in nature to analyzing and commenting on political cartoons, JiTT exercises can be developed around current editorials or news stories. The best stories provide students with practice on key course concepts.

  Example: An editorial essay by economist Paul Krugman in the *New York Times* on January 9, 2009, entitled "The Obama Gap" discusses concepts such as output gaps, fiscal stimulus, the multiplier effects of changes in taxes and public spending, and the relationship between output gaps and unemployment rates, but leaves enough ambiguity to use as the basis for a JiTT exercise. A related JiTT exercise could ask students to determine the actual size of potential and actual output and the size of public spending needed (given the multiplier given in the editorial) to close the output gap. The JiTT exercise could also include a question about the short-term (boost the economy) vs. long-term (increase public debt) effects of the spending stimulus.

These kinds of questions are at the heart of modern economic policy debates and promote engaged citizenry as well as the learning of economic ideas.

- **Tell a story.** This type of question is not typically employed by economists but is particularly helpful when students need practice applying a concept in different contexts.

  Example: A friend is writing a science fiction novel and she hires you to be the economics consultant. You remember that's how Alan Greenspan got his start, so you agree. In this novel set in the future, the air is so polluted that people must buy air like they buy water or gasoline today. The author wants a conflict to arise in which one company has a monopoly on air. She wants to write an interesting and complex novel in which outcomes aren't simple or predictable. What do you tell her?

  You can see that this type of question is likely to engage students in a way much different than typical textbook end-of-the-chapter exercises, yet promote the practice of important economic concepts.

- **Link students' current understanding with prior knowledge using structured prompts.** This type of JiTT question is useful when students need assistance in placing their thoughts in the context of existing academic discourse. As Graff & Berkenstein (2005) point out, good writing (and thinking) usually require that students link their current understanding with prior knowledge—either their own previous thinking or ideas put forward by others. The explicit "I thought . . . , Now I know . . ." and "Although . . ." structures advocated by Graff & Berkenstein (and illustrated below) encourage students to engage in a dialogue with other ideas right at the start of their essay.

Example: Students are given the following prompt about a specific course topic: "Before reading this section I thought _____, now I know_____, and this is important because _____." Note that the last part of this prompt is important because it helps avoid answers such as, "Before I didn't know what elasticity meant, now I know that it is measured by the formula . . ." Instead, a student will need to add: "Before I thought that price increases caused people to buy less of things, a simple and obvious observation, but now I know that it is important to measure how much less people buy when prices rise. This is important for companies that are thinking of raising prices."

Example: You can also use an "Although" prompt to ask, "Although most people believe _____ because _____, in fact _____ is true because _____." This type of prompt encourages students to compare and contrast naïve beliefs with more well-reasoned views or perhaps reflect on changes in their own thinking after being introduced to new economic ideas.

- **Take on a role: Imagine that . . .** Similar to "Tell a story" JiTT exercises, these types of questions promote flexibility in applying economic concepts while encouraging practice. Learning theory emphasizes that students need repeated practice with new concepts in different contexts to promote deep and long-lasting learning.

    Example: Imagine that a friend is about to marry someone from Sweden. The friend asks you, as an economics student, whether the couple should live in the United States or in Sweden based on the relative economic prospects in each country (they will consider language, cultural, and other issues separately). Write a letter to the couple explaining which country they should choose and why.

    Example: Imagine that you are a newspaper reporter assigned to write a story about the upcoming meeting of the Federal Reserve's Open Market Committee. Make a list of three questions that you will want to ask. For each question, explain carefully why it is important and what answers you expect from the Committee.

USING JiTT RESPONSES IN CLASS

As noted by others in this volume, student learning is enhanced when students' responses to JiTT questions are explicitly used to inform in-class instruction, whether through straightforward analysis or summary of JiTT responses by the instructor or through more involved follow-up in which JiTT responses are used as the basis for collaborative, small-group activities. In fact, we believe that the in-class component of the Just-in-Time pedagogy is one of the most important, although it is often given less emphasis than the development of JiTT questions. It signals to students that their work is an integral part of the learning process in the course and targets student learning difficulties identified in the JiTT responses. Both aspects provide important motivation for ongoing student engagement in the JiTT exercises throughout the semester.

The challenge of implementing meaningful in-class exercises linked to students' JiTT responses is that the responses are typically available only hours before class, giving the instructor relatively little time (compared to traditional lectures) to organize and develop related exercises. The best advice, especially for instructors new to JiTT, is to use students' JiTT responses to modify currently-used exercises and activities. Over time, the practice of efficiently developing in-class exercises that directly incorporate and target students' JiTT responses becomes a natural part of the teaching process.

Using Students' JiTT Responses at the Start of Class

When students walk into our classrooms, the first thing they will often see is a small set of JiTT responses digitally displayed on the front wall of the classroom. When class begins, we use the responses to initiate the day's presentation, reviewing what students should know as they begin the session or perhaps highlighting particularly insightful, surprising, or unique student responses. By itself, this use of students' JiTT responses has the effect of transforming the learning environment in the classroom. Students see their own work driving classroom discussion and see the professor adapting classroom teaching based on identified learning needs. The effect on the classroom learning environment is energizing. We encourage classroom discussion of the responses, targeting specific economics-related learning gaps, often leading to spirited discussions that would otherwise be missing in a more traditional lecture-based classroom.

We display student responses anonymously, usually exactly as written, on occasion omitting information that would identify an individual student or could be embarrassing. Sometimes we correct surface writing errors made by ESL students, again to avoid embarrassment. We inform students that their JiTT responses may be used in class but do not ask permission each time we use a response, although when we are concerned that a response was particularly personal, we ask permission to use it. Our experience is that students are pleased to see their own work displayed to their peers—sometimes claiming ownership even when the response is used to indicate an error in thinking. Of course, if student responses are to be used outside of the classroom, say for research on teaching and learning, then student permission is needed even if the response is used without attribution. For example, all student responses included in this chapter were obtained with formal written informed consent through a process approved by the Institutional Review Boards (IRB) at our universities.[3]

In addition to improving student understanding of economics concepts, economics instructors can also use JiTT exercises to promote the writing skills of students by using Microsoft Word to display students' JiTT responses. The in-line error-checking feature of Word underlines words that are misspelled and phrases that are grammatically incorrect. Our general experience is that recognition by students that their work may be shared in class, even without attribution, helps to improve the quality of their writing, even when the economics concepts may reveal conceptual misunderstandings. Of course, instructors must be sensitive to the general writing skills of students in their courses, especially those of non-native English writers, to avoid embarrassment. As a result, individual instructors will need to determine whether this secondary aspect of JiTT exercises should be employed and/or emphasized in their classes.

Using Students' JiTT Responses to Develop In-class Collaborative Learning Exercises

JiTT responses can also be integrated more deeply into classroom instruction by highlighting common errors that students made or by contrasting differing answers or approaches to problems. For example, if the topic warrants, we may stop the lecture to ask students to evaluate a JiTT response using the think-pair-share technique, in which students first think about a problem individually, then discuss the problem with a partner, and finally share their group responses with the whole class using personal response systems, a colored-card system, or simply by raising hands. In addition, a few students may be asked to explain their answers.[4]

JiTT responses also provide ready-to-go and often quite appropriate materials for more structured cooperative learning activities. For example, a group of three or four students may be asked to evaluate two contrasting student JiTT responses, or groups of students may be asked to develop a "model" response to the JiTT question using a subset of students' responses, none of which are completely correct. A variety of non-discipline-specific pedagogies have been developed that promote collaborative learning among students—what is unique here are the specific student responses from out-of-class JiTT exercises and their incorporation in the specific in-class activities. A specific example is provided below.

JiTT Exercise. Here we make use of one of the JiTT examples illustrated in the last section and indicate how student responses to this exercise can be used in the classroom as part of a small-group exercise. This exercise might be used during the first week of an introductory economics course to introduce students to the concept of modeling in economics and translating verbal descriptions of those models into graphical representations. The JiTT exercise is the following:

> Develop a verbal model to explain the relationship between two variables that describe the behavior of an activity related to your own personal experience (e.g. time spent studying and your grade on the upcoming exam). Also, how would you illustrate your model graphically? What would the graph look like?

Student Responses. Sample student responses (shown in class and in this case, perhaps provided as a handout in class—note that misspellings and grammatical errors are intentionally not corrected) are shown below:

Model 1: I have been working in a restaurant-eatery for a few months now and I have been noticing that when the employees smile a lot to customers, the most likely they are to get big tips. The smiler we are, the more money we get. Graphically I would put on the Y-axis the amount of tips left by customers and on the X-axis I would put the "average of smile" form the workers. The bigger this number is, the upper the line goes, at least for a while. After, even if the numbers of smile is still going up, the amount of tips left does not increase as much.

Model 2: If I put in more hours at my job, I would make more money. And therefore I will have some extra money to spend on what I want. In my situation variable 1 is hours spent working and variable 2 is wages earned. In this situation there is a positive relationship because if hours spent working is increased then wages earned will also increase. In the graph there will be an upward curve that will continue to go up.

Model 3: My day is just not long enough to accomplish everything that I want to accomplish. There is an opportunity cost for everything that I do. I have noticed that if I do not spend any time with my girlfriend that our relationship suffers. My girlfriend is not happy if everyday I do not at least call her (15 minutes). If I see her (1 hour) she continues to be even more happier. However after an hour while her enjoyment contiunues to grow, it is at a slower rate. After 3 hours, her enjoyment stops growing and begins to decrease. This model has allowed me to maximize her enjoyment without increasing my opportunity costs. For example I have to eat so I have lunch with her 1 hour. The increasing opportunity cost of having to spend more time with my girlfriend for her to get the same amount of enjoyment occurs at the one hour mark and increases at the two hour mark. As we get closer to three hours I know that the rate at which the increasing opportunity costs grows until at the three hour mark her enjoyment actually decreases. Yes with Economic Models even personal issues can be studied and handled much more effectively. From now on I will spend only one hour a day with my girlfriend and spend the other two hours studying Economics.

Model 4: An example of a model that explain the relationship between two variables that describe the behavior of an activity related is as a manager of a jewelry store, I'm able to determined the sales differences when we hired more Spanish/English speaking sales assoicates and decreases the number of employee that speak English only. The increase of both Spanish and English speaking increases our sales. A bar graph is a graphical model that describes the situation in a clear manner. On the x-axis, it would be the number of Spanish/English speaker and on the y-axis would be the sales amount. By looking at the bar graph, the bar tend to move up as we increases the number of Spanish/English speaker. Therefore, there would be a slope going upward, showing that there's a increase of sales as we increase more Spanish/English speaker.

The following activity incorporating these responses can be used as a think-pair-share activity (Millis & Cottell, 1998, pp. 72–8) or could be used as the basis for a more structured cooperative learning activity that might include groups of up to four students.

In-class Activity. The following activity could be used in class to provide additional practice with the modeling concepts introduced in this exercise.

Pick one of the models described in the responses and answer the following questions:

1. Based on the information in the verbal model you selected, draw a graph illustrating the cause-effect relationship being described. Describe your graph in terms of the example. What implications about the cause-effect relationship can you draw from this graph? Why?
2. In what ways is the cause-effect relationship described in the verbal model affected by the level of the activity? Is the cause-effect relationship described in the verbal model weaker/stronger, or even reversed as the level of the activity (the cause) increases?
3. What is unclear about the verbal model description that affects your ability to draw the corresponding graph? Explain briefly. How could the description be improved?
4. Is it easier to understand the cause-effect relationship from the verbal presentation or the graph you have constructed? Why?

After answering the questions individually, pair up with another student (or with other group members, in formal groups of more than two students) and share/discuss answers. What new insights did you gain from sharing/discussing with your partner (or group members)?

This exercise would be followed by sharing some examples with the full class, perhaps asking a few students to come to the board/overhead/tablet PC to draw the graph corresponding to one of the verbal models and explain the cause-effect relationship with respect to the graphical representation.

As you can see, the in-class activities need not be complex or involve a large amount of class time. The activity above could be conducted in as little as 15 minutes (with verbal reporting-out of group summaries) or as much as 30–50 minutes (including student displays of selected graphs and accompanying explanations), depending on the degree of student understanding and time constraints in the class. Exercises such as this explicitly link students' out-of-class JiTT exercises and in-class activities in a way that is directly related to course learning objectives (in this case, understanding cause-effect relationships, the notion of modeling these relationships, and translating those models into a graphical representation) and explicitly address multiple means of student learning. In addition, they build up relationships among students within the course that can be extended out of class to promote student study groups for exams or course projects.

DOES JiTT WORK IN ECONOMICS?

At this point, you may be encouraged to try JiTT pedagogy in your own economics course, using JiTT exercises to structure students' out-of-class studying, uncover pre/misconceptions, and inform the structure of your in-class learning environment. But the question remains, "Does JiTT work in economics?" As other authors in this volume have shown, JiTT is a powerful tool for improving learning in a variety of disciplinary contexts and has been used most extensively in science disciplines. Based on our personal experience and formal investigation, we believe that JiTT is also a particularly useful tool for improving both teaching and learning in economics. Why? First, we note that student submission rates for JiTT exercises are quite high, averaging 80–90% in our courses. Because of this, student preparation for classes is higher than before we instituted JiTT, a claim supported by student feedback on end-of-course evaluation forms. The following response is typical: "The JiTT assignments prepared me for class. It allowed me to read ahead so that I would fully understand in class the next period."

As noted in Simkins & Maier (2004), formal statistical analysis of learning outcomes of introductory economics students showed a small, positive effect of JiTT exercises on student exam performance. Qualitative data obtained as part of that project provided additional support for this result. More than two-thirds of economics students completing end-of-course surveys at Glendale Community College indicated that completing JiTT exercises during the course was more influential in their decision to read the textbook than reviewing for tests or understanding class lectures. In other words, JiTT caused students to use the textbook as a learning tool, behavior that does not always take place on its own, especially at a community college. In addition, students at North Carolina A&T State University were asked to rank ten course-related activities in terms of their "aid to learning" and "effort required." JiTT exercises ranked fourth in terms of "aid to learning," behind homework assignments, class lectures, and in-class activities, but had the highest learning-to-effort ratio of any course activity. In other words, students found JiTT to be a particularly efficient aid to their learning, providing the biggest "bang" for their studying "buck."

More generally, as noted in earlier sections, JiTT pedagogy is consistent with the seven principles for effective undergraduate teaching summarized by Chickering & Gamson, as well as the more recent learning sciences findings summarized in *How People Learn* (Bransford, Cocking & Brown, 2000). In addition, we note the following practical benefits of adopting and implementing JiTT teaching practices: (1) student responses to JiTT exercises provide valuable insights on the student learning process, allowing instructors to "get inside students' heads," and inform classroom teaching "just in time" while there is still time to address conceptual difficulties; (2) use of students' responses to JiTT questions makes class more fun for both students and instructors and often generates examples that are relevant to students, leading to increased motivation for further learning; and (3) JiTT can easily be combined with other teaching practices that have been shown to be effective in economics and other disciplines, resulting in cumulative learning effects that may be greater than those obtained by any of the teaching practices alone.

SUMMARY

As in other disciplines highlighted in this volume, JiTT provides a powerful teaching and learning tool for economists looking to improve the economic reasoning skills of their students, especially in introductory courses, where JiTT arguably has its biggest impact. JiTT not only assists students with the learning process but also provides valuable insights into students' thinking processes, which in turn can be used by instructors to improve both what and how they teach. The flexibility of the JiTT approach means that it can be used with a variety of course concepts and skills and can be easily combined with other teaching methods to provide a variety of learning experiences for economics students. Although JiTT does require some additional effort to analyze and process student responses to JiTT questions, the use of web-based course management systems such as Blackboard and Moodle help to keep this task manageable for a single instructor, even in classes with more than a hundred students. Overall, we have found that the marginal benefits of JiTT pedagogy far exceed the marginal costs—in terms of deepening our own understanding of students' economic thinking processes, providing students with additional practice on targeted course concepts, developing student motivation and engagement in the learning process, and promoting independent, metacognitive learners.

Notes

1. Our work adapting JiTT for economics education was supported by National Science Foundation grant DUE #00-88303 (2001), *Developing and Implementing Just-in-Time-Teaching (JiTT) Techniques in the Principles of Economics Course*. National surveys conducted during the 1990s indicated that economists relied heavily

on passive lecture-style teaching pedagogy, an instructional format that, according to Becker & Watts (1998, p. 4), was "established by convenience, custom, and inertia rather than efficiency or, especially, by what represents effective teaching practices in today's undergraduate curriculum." The most recent survey (Becker & Watts, 2007) suggests that there have been only minor changes in pedagogical practice in economics in the last decade.

2. Additional examples of JiTT exercises are available at the *JiTT Digital Library* <http://jittdl.physics.iupui.edu/sign_on/> and at the *Starting Point-Teaching Economics* site <http://serc.carleton.edu/econ/index.html>. Both sites were developed with National Science Foundation support (DUE# 0333646 and DUE# 0817382).

3. Instructors who would like more information about obtaining IRB approval and informed consent procedures for using their students' JiTT responses as part of public scholarship of teaching and learning research can contact the authors of this chapter using the email addresses provided in the preface. Using student responses for personal assessment of teaching effectiveness does not require IRB approval or informed consent.

4. See the chapters in this volume by Maier & Simkins (chapter 4) and Watkins & Mazur (chapter 3) for additional ideas on complementary in-class pedagogical methods that can be used in conjunction with JiTT.

References

Becker, W. E. & Watts, M. W. (2007). *A little more than chalk and talk: Results from a third national survey of teaching methods in undergraduate economics courses.* Retrieved from William E. Becker Working Papers Web site: http://mypage .iu.edu/~beckerw/working_papers.htm

Becker, W. E. & Watts, M. W. (1998). Teaching economics: What was, is, and could be. In W. Becker & M. Watts (Eds.) *Teaching economics to undergraduates – Alternatives to chalk and talk.* (pp. 1–10). Northampton MA: Edward Elgar.

Bransford, J. D., Brown, A. L., & Cocking, R. (Eds.). (2000). *How people learn: Brain, mind, experience, and school.* Washington, D.C.: National Academy Press.

Chickering, A. W. & Gamson, Z. F. (1987). Seven principles for good practice in undergraduate education. *American Association for Higher Education Bulletin, 39* (7), 3–7.

Graff, G. & Birkenstein, C. (2005). *They say/I say: The moves that matter in academic writing.* New York: W. W. Norton.

Millis, B. J. & Cottell, P. G., Jr. (1998). *Cooperative learning for higher education faculty.* Westport: Oryx Press.

Simkins, Scott P. & Maier, M. H. (2004). Using just-in-time teaching techniques in the principles of economics course. *Social Science Computer Review, 22*(4), 444–456.

9

Using Just-in-Time Teaching in History

David Pace and Joan Middendorf

If only, I told myself, there were "answers" in the humanities—if only the kinds of discrete and specific solutions that exist in physics were a part of disciplines like history—the JiTT "warmup" exercises would solve so many problems.

Initial reaction of a historian to Just-in-Time Teaching

The response above is an understandable reaction to Just-in-Time Teaching (JiTT). The applicability of JiTT teaching strategies developed for use in physics to humanities courses is not immediately obvious. Teaching in science, technology, engineering, and math (STEM) fields such as physics is organized largely around well-understood conceptual ideas and concrete problems with discrete solutions. Scholars working in fields such as history, by contrast, are accustomed to presenting conflicting interpretations of ambiguous phenomena. Students majoring in the sciences may not encounter contested interpretations until they are well into their undergraduate or even their graduate careers; those in the humanities often deal with discipline-based controversy on their first day of class.

These problems are particularly vexing in history, a discipline in which the essay exam remains the gold standard of pedagogical assessment. The *bête noire* of historians in higher education is high school history tests that use multiple-choice items to measure students' ability to memorize long lists of facts about the past. In contrast, for history professors, the real task of the history student is to learn how to marshal evidence to support sophisticated interpretations of complex and often ambiguous issues. This chapter demonstrates how we use JiTT exercises in combination with the "decoding the disciplines" method (Middendorf & Pace, 2004, 2006). In particular, we highlight ways in which JiTT exercises can develop increasingly more complex historical thinking skills throughout a semester-long undergraduate course. We conclude with an assessment of JiTT's effectiveness in promoting student learning in humanities courses.

USING JiTT IN HISTORY: BACKGROUND

JiTT exercises, as noted in other chapters in this volume, include one or more questions covering upcoming course material that students are required to answer and submit online a few hours before class. The exercises, designed to help students gain an understanding of new concepts or practice new skills, are most effective when students work in their "zone of proximal development," Vygotsky's (1978) term to describe how the best learning takes place just beyond what the learner already knows. Students' responses to the JiTT questions help an instructor figure out what the learners know or can do so that they can be brought to the next level. JiTT exercises are an occasion for students to make useful mistakes and provide valuable feedback to both instructors and students about where to concentrate teaching and learning efforts in a course.

To history instructors steeped in the tradition of complex interpretation, the JiTT methodology may seem to betray their disciplinary culture. How, they may ask, can the intricacy of a historical argument be reduced to a simple question with a single answer? Such a question, of course, rests on a misunderstanding of the nature of JiTT, which should focus on the process by which a student reaches an answer, rather than the answer itself. But the question does point to a central challenge: how can humanities instructors break the complex tasks that they wish their students to complete into discrete operations? So long as humanists treat their disciplines as a mystical entity that must be intuited spontaneously in a burst of Zen-like enlightenment, it will be difficult to make use of the valuable insights that might be derived from the application of JiTT principles to their disciplines. As a result, instructors may overlook a potentially valuable teaching tool for improving student learning.

USING JUST-IN-TIME TEACHING TO DECODE A DISCIPLINE

Before JiTT can be applied in the humanities, instructors in these fields must first systematically break apart the complex reasoning processes dominant in their disciplines to define more precisely the specific operations that students must master to operate successfully in the field, a process that we call "decoding the disciplines." As Shulman (2002) notes, teaching and learning methods are most likely domain-specific; consequently, the task of deconstructing the disciplinary reasoning processes will be different for each humanities discipline. It is in identifying the concepts and skills of a specific discipline that the merger of JiTT and the decoding the disciplines approach can greatly

DECODING THE DISCIPLINES:
Seven Steps to Overcome Obstacles to Learning

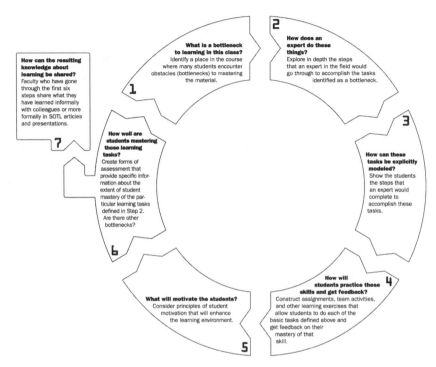

How can the resulting knowledge about learning be shared? Faculty who have gone through the first six steps share what they have learned informally with colleagues or more formally in SOTL articles and presentations. **7**

What is a bottleneck to learning in this class? Identify a place in the course where many students encounter obstacles (bottlenecks) to mastering the material. **1**

How does an expert do these things? Explore in depth the steps that an expert in the field would go through to accomplish the tasks identified as a bottleneck. **2**

How can these tasks be explicitly modeled? Show the students the steps that an expert would complete to accomplish these tasks. **3**

How will students practice these skills and get feedback? Construct assignments, team activities, and other learning exercises that allow students to do each of the basic tasks defined above and get feedback on their mastery of that skill. **4**

What will motivate the students? Consider principles of student motivation that will enhance the learning environment. **5**

How well are students mastering these learning tasks? Create forms of assessment that provide specific information about the extent of student mastery of the particular learning tasks defined in Step 2. Are there other bottlenecks? **6**

Figure 9.1. The Decoding the Disciplines Model. From Middendorf & Pace (2004). Reprinted with permission.

increase the effectiveness of both. The decoding the disciplines model leads instructors from the identification of crucial bottlenecks that hinder student learning to the creation and assessment of specific teaching strategies that make visible to students (and faculty members) the tacit mental operations that undergird specific disciplinary fields. JiTT can help scaffold that process for students in a systematic way to develop more effective and meaningful disciplinary learning.

The Decoding the Disciplines Model

The decoding the disciplines model illustrated in Figure 9.1 was developed to help instructors make explicit the thinking necessary for student success in a course. The seven-step process begins by asking an instructor to identify a bottleneck, a place in their course where large numbers of students have difficulty accomplishing a basic task. The second step calls for the instructor to identify mental operations they would undertake to get past the bottleneck. This is the most difficult part of the decoding the disciplines process because it entails breaking down tacit knowledge, something instructors do without having to consciously think about it (and that often remains hidden to students). This step of the process is undertaken through intense interviews. In the third step the instructor shows the students what the expert would do to overcome the bottleneck, and in the fourth step, the instructor provides assignments and activities that allow the students to practice these skills. While the two previous steps are going on, the instructor also considers principles of motivation to enhance learning of the identified mental operations, which is the fifth step. In the sixth step the instructor designs ways to assess whether students have mastered the identified operations. The seventh step asks instructors to undertake metacognitive reflection on what they have learned from this process and to consider ways that they might share their results with others. The process is iterative, as results with actual students may require adjustments in any of the steps. By identifying a bottleneck to learning and clarifying what a successful performance would look like, instructors are more likely to make visible to students disciplinary ways of thinking that previously remained hidden.

Using JiTT with the Decoding the Disciplines Model. JiTT methods complement several of the decoding the disciplines steps outlined above. By analyzing student responses to well-crafted JiTT questions, instructors can determine the bottlenecks where learning is impeded (Step 1). JiTT exercises provide students with practice in applying course skills and concepts, while the interactive JiTT lecture provides feedback for students on their proficiency on specific skills or concepts (Step 4). When instructors include an affective JiTT question (What did you find most confusing/difficult/interesting?) the instructor gains feedback about student motivation (Step 5). JiTT exercises can also be used to assess how well students are learning (Step 6), providing valuable feedback on student efforts at thinking and learning. Finally, the JiTT Digital Library provides instructors with an online vehicle for sharing JiTT prompts, collaborative exercises, and related course materials (Step 7).[1]

USING JiTT IN HISTORY: A CASE STUDY

David Pace (co-author of this chapter) teaches the course, *Visions of the Future: A History*, annually to a class of 60–100 students, most of whom are in their first year of college. The primary course goal is to compare beliefs about the future in different periods of history in order to explore changes in attitudes toward religion, science, technology, popular culture, consumerism, war, and the environment. To achieve this goal, the course emphasizes "thinking historically" rather than studying a specific historical period.

Thinking like a Historian: The Use of Evidence

A key element in most undergraduate history courses is the use of evidence to support a particular interpretation of the past. The concept of "evidence" common to professional historians is very different than the notion of "facts" held by many undergraduates. For historians, facts are independent units of truth whose importance is assured by their having actually occurred, while evidence is always relative to a particular argument. Evidence is of importance only because it serves to make more or less likely a particular interpretation of the past. The factual basis for evidence is of course important, but the evidence itself is of use only when it is linked through systematic argument to a particular position.

This distinction between facts and evidence is so obvious to most historians that they rarely teach it explicitly. However, the failure to understand this difference can lead to disastrous results for students. For example, undergraduates are likely to fail if they believe that the task on an essay test is merely to "download" all the facts remotely suggested by the question. Even after it has been explained in class, the distinction between regurgitating lists of memorized facts and generating systematic historical arguments, tacitly understood by professional historians, remains unclear to many students. Therefore, helping students master the historians' use and understanding of evidence is a necessary step in removing bottlenecks to learning in these courses.

It is here that JiTT techniques are especially useful. By using JiTT exercises regularly throughout the semester, instructors can repeatedly model the process of "historical thinking" while giving students multiple opportunities to practice and receive feedback on their ability to use evidence. In a JiTT exercise used during the second week of the course, for example, students are asked to identify a passage from a particular secondary source that might be useful in an essay and explain how this passage might be used in the essay. That JiTT exercise is reproduced below:

> Imagine that you were preparing to write an essay on the ways that Christians in various ages reinterpreted the Book of Revelation and other biblical prophesies of the end of the world in terms of the issues of their own time.

1. Find a short passage in the excerpts from Walter Klaassen's *Living at the End of the Ages* in the course reader that might be useful as evidence in such an essay.
2. Briefly explain how this passage might be used in the hypothetical essay suggested above. (In other words, what does it tell us that might serve as evidence in a discussion of the ways biblical prophecy has been used in various periods?)
3. Find a short passage from the examples of the apocalyptic writing available on the Web site that that might be useful as evidence in the essay described above.
4. Briefly explain how this passage might be used in the hypothetical essay suggested above. (In other words what does it tell us that might serve as evidence in a discussion of the ways biblical prophecy has been used in various periods?)

After students submit their JiTT responses, usually a few hours before class, instructors analyze these responses to identify student difficulties so that they can be addressed in the upcoming class. For example, in the JiTT exercise highlighted above, most students were good at selecting a passage of evidence but they did not make a good case for how the evidence might be used. Most of them simply restated the passage, as in the following JiTT answer:

> In "Gregory to Ethelbert, King of the Angels (June 601)," the passage describes the fact that things that may be happening now in nature are actually signs that the world is ending.

Only about 10% of the students were able to successfully describe how the passage of evidence might be used, as illustrated in the following JiTT response:

> This outlines the typical apocalyptic signs and can be used as an analogous instance to past points in time when the same apocalyptic thoughts were being applied to a different era.

To respond to the identified learning gap, the instructor addressed this issue in the upcoming class, while subsequent JiTT exercises provided additional practice for students, each time with a slightly different historical context. A single attempt at a complex operation is rarely sufficient. Weekly JiTT warmups provide students with necessary reinforcement. For example, in the third week of the course students are asked to identify passages that might be useful as examples of patterns in the primary texts being studied, and in the fourth week they are asked to find passages that exemplify some of the essential differences between two thinkers and explain what characteristics of these passages serve this purpose.

The learning implicit in these JiTT exercises is reinforced in other elements of the course. Examples of the process of identifying relevant bits of evidence to support particular assertions are explicitly presented in lectures. Collaborative learning teams are presented in class with exercises involving the same skills. In addition, material on the course Web site describes the process of reading selectively in search of relevant evidence, including a recording of the instructor thinking aloud about the relevance of various sections of a short reading passage as he himself reads through this secondary source.

Getting Beyond Surface Learning

Historical analysis involves more than simply matching a hypothesis with written evidence to provide explicit examples of the occurrence of a particular phenomenon. Historians are as interested in what is implicit in a source as in what is explicitly and consciously presented. Therefore, once students have begun to understand the need to identify relevant evidence as opposed to memorizing facts, it is necessary to expand their notion of what it means to "read" evidence. They must learn to look not only for what a source literally "says" to support or attack a particular argument, but also what assumptions and values underlie this artifact.

The notion that there are values and assumptions implicit in a historical source is a very demanding concept that must be carefully explored in multiple ways, including lectures, hands-on in-class cooperative learning exercises, and course Web site resources. However, JiTT exercises provide students with the most useful practice with the idea of assumptions implicit in historical evidence. For example, during the fourth week students are asked to read a passage from Marx and:

a) summarize the argument in this particular primary source;
b) identify one assumption made by the author;
c) provide a short passage in which this assumption was present; and
d) explain what about this passage convinced them that it was good evidence of this particular assumption.

In the following week students are asked to identify one value or assumption that Marx shared with Condorcet (an early proponent of progress studied in an earlier week). Again they are asked to provide a passage from each in which the assumption or value was detectable and to explain what about the passage convinced them that it was a good example of this particular assumption or value. Next, they are asked to repeat the entire process, this time focusing on a value or assumption that distinguished Marx from Condorcet. This is followed the next week by a JiTT exercise that asks students to go through a similar process contrasting the values of supporters and skeptics of the value of progress.

These skills are necessary for the kinds of analysis required in a history course and they must be repeated frequently to become a natural part of students' historical thinking processes, mimicking the thinking processes of professional historians. However, it is also necessary that students understand when it is appropriate to employ these skills, and to have experience at using them in the process of answering a real historical question. Moreover, to motivate students it is useful to remind them that these skills will help them succeed in the larger-stake tasks of the course, such as answering exam questions. JiTT exercises can be invaluable in giving students an opportunity to practice this kind of integration of skills in a global task. Thus the JiTT exercise for the sixth week begins by asking students to imagine that they are preparing to write a history paper on the role of science and technology in promoting human well-being:

> Imagine that you were writing an essay comparing nineteenth and twentieth-century thinkers who believed that science and technology would greatly improve the quality of human life with those who believed that this kind of progress was irrelevant or even detrimental to human happiness.

This exercise requires students to go through many of the steps necessary to successfully write a paper on this topic: identify individuals with contrasting positions, specify the nature of their differences, and compare the value systems and sets of assumptions that underlay each position. The JiTT exercise gives them an opportunity to synthesize these skills and gain confidence in the process of developing historical arguments in a relatively low-stakes environment while there is still time for feedback and additional practice. That is, this JiTT exercise, like others in the course, provides a type of intellectual scaffolding for students as they build independent thinking, writing, and analysis skills that are necessary to be successful in the course.

ASSESSING THE IMPACT OF JiTT ON STUDENT LEARNING

To determine the relationship between student learning in the course and the efficacy of JiTT methods we used a form of pre-course and post-course testing. At the beginning and end of the semester students were given the same set of questions designed to assess their mastery of specific skills. The student responses were coded, combined, and randomized before they were made available to the instructor. The instructor then used a grading rubric to assign points to each answer without knowing whether a particular answer had been given at the beginning or the end of the course. Next, the average pre- and post-scores were compared. Of all the skills measured in the assessment, the ability to identify appropriate evidence demonstrated the greatest change. As a group, students improved by 26% in this area over the course of the semester. Because this skill was the one most frequently presented in the JiTT exercises, it is likely that the JiTT exercises had a positive impact on this result.

More research needs to be done to understand the behavior of students who fall behind in courses that implement the JiTT strategy, as well as those whose effort on JiTT exercises varies across the semester. Clearly, JiTT requires a sustained weekly effort throughout the semester, a style of studying that many students are not accustomed to in traditionally-taught courses. It would be useful to better understand why a small number of students seem to resist the JiTT process or do not seem to make the effort required (at least on a consistent basis) to adequately complete the JiTT exercises (or attempt them at all). Camp, Middendorf, & Sullivan (chapter 2) provide additional insights about student motivation and ways to promote continuing engagement by students in the JiTT process throughout the course.

CONCLUSION

The combination of the Decoding the Disciplines approach and JiTT offered a powerful tool for increasing learning in a history class. Decoding the Disciplines was used to break complex historical thinking skills down into component parts while JiTT exercises provided the scaffolding and redundancy necessary for students to internalize these sophisticated thinking skills. JiTT exercises were used in a systematic, sequential manner to model skills for students, to provide students opportunities for practice and feedback, and to assess student learning.

Our assessments showed that students performed significantly better on a post-test and that there was a strong correlation between student performance on weekly JiTT exercises and essay exams. Further research, both in history and other disciplines, is needed to understand the effects of JiTT on low scoring students and to investigate why students' performances varied widely on the JiTT exercises.

Note

1. The JiTT Digital Library is accessible at http://jittdl.physics.iupui.edu/sign_on/.

References

Middendorf, J. & Pace, D. (2006). Decoding the disciplines: A model for drawing faculty into SoTL. Poster presented at the International Scholarship of Teaching and Learning Conference. (November) Washington, DC.

Middendorf, J. & Pace, D. (Eds.). (2004). Decoding the disciplines: Helping students learn disciplinary ways of thinking. *New Directions for Teaching and Learning*, 98. San Francisco: Jossey-Bass.

Shulman, L. (2002). Forward. In M. Huber & S. Morreale (Eds.), Disciplinary styles in the scholarship of teaching and learning. Washington: American Association for Higher Education.

Vygotsky, L. S. (1978). *Mind in society: The development of higher psychological processes* (M. Cole, V. John-Steiner, S. Scribner, & E. Souberman, Eds. & Trans.). Cambridge, MA: Harvard University Press.

10

Using Just-in-Time Teaching to Foster Critical Thinking in a Humanities Course

Claude Cookman

Just-in-Time Teaching (JiTT) has helped me harness the power of active learning to systematically promote critical thinking in a humanities course that I teach at Indiana University, *The History of Twentieth Century Photography*. In this chapter I describe my use of JiTT in this course and offer quantitative and qualitative data on the impact of JiTT on my students' learning. Although my examples throughout refer to a specific course, they illustrate more broadly how a teaching innovation originally developed for physics education and used widely in science, technology, engineering, and math (STEM) disciplines can be adapted for use in humanities courses.

Although my specific use of JiTT differs from most of the other authors in this book, the essential characteristics that make JiTT a powerful teaching and learning tool are present: use of carefully designed sets of questions requiring a Web-based response by students hours before class and analysis of the responses by the instructor prior to class to inform classroom teaching. In my own experience, I have found that JiTT is an effective means for motivating and engaging students in the humanities, fostering critical thinking in the liberal arts tradition.

In this chapter I first describe the characteristics of *The History of Twentieth Century Photography* course and the learning objectives that underlie my teaching strategies in this course. Next, I summarize my adaptation of the JiTT pedagogy, in particular the intentional use of reading exercises that serve as a focal point in this course. In the last section I discuss students' assessment of JiTT as a learning tool, along with modifications that I have made in my own use of JiTT in response to student feedback.

IMPLEMENTING JiTT IN A HUMANITIES COURSE: BACKGROUND

The History of Twentieth Century Photography course is taught in a large-lecture format, typically enrolling about 150 students primarily from the School of Fine Arts, which requires the course for majors in the Bachelor and Master of Fine Arts photography programs, and from the School of Journalism, which credits it as a core research requirement. The course surveys photography as a medium of art and communication, examining the art genres of portraiture, landscape, and the nude, and such communication categories as war photography, the social documentary tradition, the magazine picture story, and fashion photography. The course also explores the effects of technology and situates more than 125 photographers and their work in historical and social contexts. Finally, the course considers how postmodern theory has changed our understanding of the photograph and the photographic act.

I use JiTT to foster critical thinking, which I define in the syllabus as: (1) learning to read critically—to identify an author's thesis and arguments and then evaluate whether those arguments convincingly support her or his conclusions, and (2) practicing a variety of mental operations that are crucial to studying visual art and practicing art history, including observing, describing, comparing and contrasting, summarizing, classifying, analyzing, synthesizing, interpreting, sourcing, periodizing, contextualizing, and formulating and testing a thesis. In addition to JiTT, I draw on a variety of pedagogical theories and research to create a student learning environment that promotes active, critical thinking, including Barr & Tagg's (1995) focus on student learning, Perry's (1970) research on the intellectual and ethical development of college students, Chickering & Gamson's (1987) principles of effective teaching practices, and Bloom's (1956) taxonomy of cognitive learning objectives.

Distilled from my own practices as a historian of photography, the mental operations listed above as critical to the course are an attempt to concretize critical thinking within my discipline. Donald (2002) points out that although some critical thinking skills might be generic, students must also master discipline-specific modes of thinking. In effect, I teach a methodology for practicing the history of photography, not just the discipline's domain content. Faculty who struggle to cover the ever-growing content in their fields may question the wisdom of teaching methodology to aspiring photographers who have no interest in becoming historians. In my experience, however, giving students the methodological tools to construct their own history of photography motivates them to learn the domain knowledge at a deeper level.

With this teaching and learning philosophy in mind, the syllabus lists five other domain-specific student learning objectives for the course. By the end of the course students should:

- acquire broad knowledge of twentieth century photography.
- acquire deep knowledge of a specific photographer, movement, or issue.
- learn to articulate intellectual, aesthetic, and emotional responses to photographs.
- develop the interest and skills necessary for lifelong learning of the history of photography.
- acquire a historical consciousness.

To accomplish these objectives, I have designed a writing-intensive course in which JiTT plays a central role.[1]

USING JiTT IN THE HUMANITIES: THINKING ABOUT THE READINGS (TARs) ASSIGNMENTS

I call my JiTT exercises TARs, which is an acronym for "Thinking About the Readings." Typically, each TAR assignment includes two questions that students must answer online prior to the upcoming class in which the topic will be discussed. Instructions on the first TAR assignment include a note to students about the importance of TAR assignments in developing critical thinking skills in the course. The note, shown below, also sets expectations about the quality of TAR responses:

> As explained in the syllabus, the primary objective of TAR assignments is to help you become better critical thinkers. Writing is a way of making our thinking concrete and tangible. Often the process of writing generates new thought. The primary expectation for your TAR assignments flows directly from this objective. You must demonstrate that you have thought deeply about the readings—that you have identified and understood the authors' primary ideas and that you have generated your own ideas in response to theirs.

It is important that students understand the purpose of TARs in my course from the outset. Students need to know that they are not just busy work, but rather form a series of structured exercises to build critical thinking skills in a sequential manner during the semester. Further, they are used in conjunction with other writing assignments, which build in cognitive complexity throughout the course. It is also critically important that students actively participate in these exercises from the start and remain engaged throughout the course. Following Duffy and Jonassen's (1992) insight that students should actively construct knowledge—an idea also emphasized in the learning sciences literature (Bransford, Brown, & Cocking, 2000)—I explain that TARs are really about students constructing their own history of twentieth century photography.

The idea is to have students formulate their own position and justify it in writing; there are no right or wrong answers, although some answers may be better than others. This view is problematic for many students, especially those new to college, who may see knowledge in a much more objective way. To provide practice with the skill of reasoned discourse, the TAR assignments are graduated to build students' critical thinking skills incrementally, demanding higher skill levels as the semester progresses. Some questions, especially those asking students to identify theses and evaluate arguments, are repeated throughout the course, allowing students to gain facility with specific mental operations that are particularly important in the humanities.

TAR Assignments and Bloom's Taxonomy

I use Bloom's (1956) taxonomy of cognitive objectives to structure my thinking about TAR questions and to intentionally build students' critical thinking skills in a developmental manner. To illustrate, early in the semester comprehension questions predominate TAR assignments. For example, I might ask students to summarize in their own words the readings assigned for the upcoming class session. The question below is an example of this type and is typically included as part of the first TAR of the semester:

> Pennell and Stieglitz take different positions on the major question for Pictorialism: Is photography an art? Construct an argument between the two men, summarizing their points pro and con on this issue. Also, identify the assumptions behind their definition of "art." Are they talking about the same thing? Or, are their differences primarily semantic?

Students must understand the articles deeply enough to reformulate the authors' arguments in their own words. The question also functions at the synthesis level of Bloom's taxonomy because students must interweave two sets of ideas into a single debate.

To promote the application of ideas I ask students to transfer ideas from a text by analyzing a photograph they have not seen before. One such prompt asks:

Hall identifies six elements and ten themes in the paradigm of French humanist photography. Use as many of those elements and themes as applicable to discuss this photograph.

Moving one level higher on Bloom's taxonomy to the level of analysis, I ask students to determine the strength of an argument and to identify and critique the author's hidden assumptions or unconscious blind spots. The following TAR illustrates this type of question:

"Hagiography" literally means writing about the saints. When it's applied to historians and biographers it takes on a pejorative connotation. It implies they are unduly praising, heroicizing, idolizing, or canonizing their subjects. Does Jonathan Green engage in hagiography of Robert Frank in this reading? Or, is his account of Frank justified? Say yes or no, and most importantly, defend your answer: Why or why not?

TAR assignments provide a valuable tool for developing students' cognitive skills in an intentional, systematic way. Moreover, Bloom's taxonomy provides a useful framework for developing effective sets of questions targeted at specific cognitive skills that students will use in a variety of writing assignments throughout the semester.

Although the first of the two questions in a TAR assignment always focuses on the readings for the upcoming class session, the second question sometimes asks students to express intellectual, aesthetic, or emotional responses to photographs. Early in the semester I ask students to observe a photograph, describe its contents, analyze its formal values, and interpret or construct their own meanings for it. Subsequently, I show students a dozen images by a photographer we have not discussed, asking them to write a general summary of the entire group and then analyze one image that exemplifies the group. Later in the semester, when we have established a solid base of domain-specific knowledge, I ask them to classify photographs according to their style, movement, and time period, and of course I require them to explain and justify their responses. Ultimately, students incorporate the seeing, thinking, and writing skills they acquire from these TAR assignments into their course research papers.

The Role of Oppositional Readings in TAR Assignments

Many TAR assignments are based on oppositional readings in which authors take contradictory points of view. For example, the debate surrounding a famous war photograph, Robert Capa's 1936 picture from the Spanish Civil War, entitled "Falling Soldier," has roiled photojournalism for three decades. Based on interviews with journalists, Phillip Knightley (2004) accuses Capa of staging the photograph, which purports to show a Spanish loyalist soldier at the instant he is fatally struck by a bullet. Capa's biographer Richard Whelan (2002) defends the photograph's veracity, identifying the slain soldier, marshaling evidence about the battle, and interviewing a forensic detective about the falling body.

The first question in the accompanying TAR assignment focuses on students' comprehension of the readings: "Summarize in your own words Knightley's argument that Capa staged this photograph. Summarize in your own words Whelan's argument that the photograph is authentic." The next question—"Whose argument do you find more convincing? Why?"—asks students to evaluate the arguments, pushing students to examine the very premise of the debate—that staging is somehow wrong in photojournalism. The final question in this TAR assignment asks students to address this issue directly: "In your opinion, does it matter whether or not this photograph was staged? Why or why not? This is a chance to explore and articulate your ideas about the truth value of photography." This question moves students beyond the readings, asking them to explore their beliefs about truth and photography. Perry's (1970) research on the intellectual and ethical development of college students suggests that it is important to help students recognize competing arguments, and then to begin to make a reasoned and context-appropriate commitment to one position.

The resulting responses provide valuable insights into students' thinking processes and preconceptions that otherwise might remain hidden. For example, most student art photographers argue that staging is a non-issue. Typical is this response by a senior BFA student, who argues that all photographers, including photojournalists, have a right to use any means necessary to convey their intended message:

> I do not believe that it matters a great deal whether or not the photo was staged. As a war photographer, Capa was supposed to give a visual documentation of what war was like. The Falling Soldier photo does give its audience a feel for the tragedy of war. If Capa had to set up the photo in order to make his point more effective, then the photo still serves its purpose. A staged but emotionally impacting image is more effective than a spontaneous "true" photo that is less visually arresting. . . . In all photographs, the person behind the camera makes choices to varying degrees. Even in documentary photography, the photographer should be reserved the right to edit his or her photo in order to convey the intended message.

In contrast, most student photojournalists argue that staging is not ethically acceptable. One student, who was an editor of the student newspaper, based his argument against staging on ethics, integrity and credibility:

> Truth is subjective; absolute truth may be impossible to achieve. But, in my mind, a photographer should come as close to the truth as possible in his or her images. In some ways, it doesn't matter that this photograph was staged because one could argue that if this one was staged, something that resembled this happened somewhere, and in that sense, caused some sort of truth. One could also argue that if the image were staged, this did not happen; therefore it is not true and is unethical. I tend to agree with the latter. I take the ethical standards in journalism, specifically in photography, for exactly what they are. The only thing we have as journalists is our integrity. If we sacrifice that, we are sacrificing our moral obligation to our profession and our public. If a photographer portrays something that never happened as a true event, there goes your credibility.

A common practice in the teaching of art history is to ask students to compare and contrast two works of art. The premise is that they will see more deeply by examining two approaches to the same motif. TAR assignments grounded in oppositional readings expand the compare and contrast approach to texts. Such critical thinking does not occur when students read textbooks that are full of bloodless, homogenized prose, lacking strong points of view against which students can pit their own thinking. Well-chosen oppositional readings, including artists' statements, criticism, biographies, Web-based essays, and peer-reviewed journal articles and book chapters offer authentic authorial voices that engage students in thinking through competing perspectives on a issue. Such readings offer two other values directly connected to the course's capstone assignment, the research paper. First, they require students to sample and analyze the wide range of sources available for their research projects. Second, they offer models of professional writing that students can use to improve their own writing. Seeing, reading, and analyzing examples of authentic writing helps students to develop the ability to critically assess their own work.

TAR Assignments: A Summary

The examples in this section illustrate how JiTT (TARs) can be used to intentionally build students' general and discipline-based critical thinking skills in a humanities course. Using Bloom's taxonomy of cognitive learning as a framework for their construction, TARs not only serve to build these skills generally, but also help prepare students for writing assignments and essay-type exam

questions throughout the course. TAR assignments work in tandem with traditional teaching methods and course material in the humanities, but in
addition provide valuable formative assessment of learning for both students
and instructors.

Formative Assessment and Feedback with TARs

Because TARs count for 20% of the semester grade, these assignments have a
modest summative role in assessing student learning. More importantly, however, TARs provide formative assessment of student learning for both instructors and students, indicating how well students are meeting course objectives
and preparing them for exam essay questions and research papers. Because
TARs are viewed as a developmental tool, feedback on TAR assignments is
more extensive—and more labor intensive—at the beginning of the semester.
On the first four assignments my two grading assistants and I write positive
feedback and constructive criticism to all students. We average three to four
hours per assignment, grading about 40–45 students each. Here's a portion of
the feedback for a student who scored a B on the first TAR assignment about
the Pennell-Stieglitz readings, mentioned earlier. It includes extensive suggestions for improvement on future TARs:

> Generally, a good start on your first TAR assignment, but there's room for
> improvement on future ones. We want you to demonstrate that you've read the
> articles carefully, thought about them analytically and formulated your own
> response. You show that only to a degree. You characterize Pennell's argument as:
> "He felt that during the pictorialist time photography was still too new to be true
> art. He thought it needed more recognition from people other than its main sup-
> porters." Okay, but that's only one small dimension. Pennell argued photography
> was too easy, did not require any apprenticeship, was mechanical, was practiced
> by amateurs, did not require any handwork, etc. So, I encourage you to be more
> complete in your answers. You don't have to say everything possible, but push
> yourself to go beyond this. Be especially careful that you have identified the
> author's main point, or thesis. So, I would also encourage you to read the articles
> more critically.

By the third or fourth TAR assignment most students understand the
expected level of analysis and writing, and as a result the quality of their
responses rises accordingly. For the remainder of the semester our feedback
typically shortens to a comment or two, intended to assure students that we
are reading their responses. For students who fail to show improvement in
their TAR responses, we continue to give concrete suggestions on how they

can read more critically and write more effectively. As the semester progresses, we lower the grades for students who do not show progress and for the small number of students who, after repeated warnings, do not write enough to answer the questions. At this stage in our use of TARs we average an hour to an hour and a half in grading each assignment.

Preparation for Class

One advantage of JiTT pedagogy is that I can walk into class knowing how the class divides on an issue and initiate a lively discussion. Although intense debates are expected in a small seminar format, JiTT also makes them possible in large lecture courses. For example, an animated discussion invariably occurs in my course on the question of whether Capa staged the moment-of-death photograph and whether it matters. Such engagement would be less likely to occur if students were hearing about the issue for the first time in a lecture or even if they read the material beforehand and marked it with a highlighter. JiTT requires students to think carefully about a complex issue and defend a position—prior to the classroom discussion. As a consequence, every student has an idea to contribute. Because I have reviewed their responses before class I can intentionally call on students who I know have opposing positions. On the best days, the students talk directly to each other and I can drop my role as moderator. As a result of the classroom debates some students move away from hard-line positions and push their thinking to a more nuanced view. Occasionally, a few students actually change perspectives because of the debate. Many students do not, but they have listened attentively to alternate points of view at a level that goes deeper and lasts longer than a mere lecture could achieve.

STUDENT RESPONSES TO JiTT

Data collected from this course over the 2004–2008 period indicate that students find value in the JiTT method, even though it often differs significantly from the teaching methods experienced in many of their other courses. Student responses to quantitative and open-ended questions on surveys, as well as in focus groups, support the claim that TAR assignments contribute positively to students' learning. As the figures in Table 10.1 show, a large majority of students believe that TAR assignments help them process course readings at a deeper level, enhance their critical thinking skills, and are worth the effort involved. Although self-reported, these responses are also in line with my personal observations in the course.

Table 10.1. Percentage of Students Responding "Yes" to Listed Survey Questions in 2004, 2006, and 2008

	2004 [Number of students responding = 61]	2006 [Number of students responding = 90]	2008 [Number of students responding = 76]
Did the TARs help you process the readings at a deeper level?	96.7	83.3	92.1
Did the TARs help you increase your critical thinking skills?	82.0	73.3	90.8
Did the learning you gained from the TARs make them worth the work they required?	75.4	65.0	90.8

Responding to open-ended surveys at the end of the course, many students linked TARs to the course objective of critical thinking. Others commented on how JiTT increased their motivation and engagement. Examples of student comments are shown below:

- The TARs made me think. Sometimes when I did not want to. They also made me write, which in turn made me think. It was very difficult, but very good for me.
- I thought the TARs helped to force me not to fall behind.
- Glad they were assigned—otherwise I probably wouldn't do the reading to my fullest capabilities.
- I think the TAR assignments are the most important assignments of the course. They stimulated my thinking and kept me up to date with the readings.

Many students indicated that this course required more study time than their other courses, a result they attributed to the TAR assignments. Commenting on the time commitment, one student wrote, "This class forces you to put a lot of work in—other classes expect you to but do not actually require it. I learned a lot, but stressed a lot as well." Further reflecting the mixed feelings that students had about TAR assignments, the responses to questions asking students to rate the best aspects of the course and the worst aspects of the course both included references to TAR assignments. Nevertheless, although students may not always like the continuous effort required of the JiTT method, they generally (if grudgingly) concede that the effort pays off in increased learning.

An anonymous focus group session was conducted with students at the end of the course in 2006. Asked to compare the amount of time they spent on this course with other courses, one graduate student said, "I probably coasted through college and didn't spend a lot of time reading assigned readings or studying outside of class. . . . I would say, on average, compared with my undergrad career, I spent two to three times as much time reading, writing, or refining my writing in this course." Another student said, "Not only did you have to do the readings, but you had to think about the readings in such a way that you could form an argument either for or against it. . . . You had to understand to such a level that you could write a paper almost in a thesis-argument form."

Another student credited TARs with helping her/him get a better grade: "I think if this class were tailored to have two or three exams over the content, the readings, and the lectures I think my grade would have been at least a letter grade lower." Asked why, she/he explained, "There's a certain amount of uncertainty you have when you are taking a test. There's also other factors: [I] could have had a bad day . . ." She/he also liked the autonomy that TAR assignments allowed: "TARs were [given out] several days in advance basically like a take-home essay. . . . If you had a mental block you could leave them alone, go away and come back to it when you were clearer-headed. . . . To me, I think the way it is tailored, it teaches people to teach themselves rather than trying to extract a bunch of facts." Another student mentioned the classroom dimension and its relationship to the TAR assignments: " . . . we had discussions in class that helped a lot. And so bringing all that (readings, essays, and discussion) together I learned a lot more."

MISTAKES AND LESSONS LEARNED

It is important to continually assess the effectiveness of JiTT and use the resulting information to improve its implementation. The most important lessons I have learned about JiTT resulted from mistakes I made, namely:

1. It is possible to demand too much from students, to overwhelm them and cause them to become disenchanted with the subject.

Table 10.2. Percentage of Students Who Agreed or Strongly Agreed to Listed Survey Questions, 2006 and 2008

	2006 [Number of students responding = 90]	2008 [Number of students responding = 76]
TARs helped me better understand course material.	78.1	96.1
TARs made me feel more responsible for my success.	74.7	93.4
TARs helped me keep up with reading and work.	78.0	90.8

2. Students need the clarity of specific guidelines when completing TAR assignments, including a minimum length for the responses to the TAR questions.

Table 10.2 lists responses to end-of-course student survey questions administered in both 2006 and 2008. The lowest evaluations occurred in spring 2006, when I overreached and failed to set specific expectations (also seen in Table 10.1).

Specifically, in 2006, in addition to fostering critical thinking, I used TAR assignments to promote higher and more formal writing standards. I required correct spelling, grammar, punctuation, and word usage, and stipulated a thesis-argument structure for every essay. I also declined requests by students to specify a minimum length for responses, insisting on "completeness" as the standard. My refusal stemmed partly from my belief that students should take responsibility for their own education and should write as much, or as little, as they considered valuable for their own learning. Because we reduced grades for excessively short answers, this caused understandable confusion among some students. My grading assistants embraced the writing standards with enthusiasm and early in the semester scored many students in the low 80s or below. In addition, the TAR assignments counted for 30% of the course grade that year. By the fourth assignment, many students reported feeling stressed and some were beginning to disengage from the class due to the sheer effort required.

A month into the semester I administered a course questionnaire to gain input and give students a chance to vent their frustrations. The key question was: "Does the learning you are gaining from the TAR assignments make them worth the work they require?" Of 92 students, 43.5% said yes, and 56.5%

said no. In written responses, many said they felt uncertain because of my failure to specify a minimum length and were overwhelmed by the combined demands of the reading, writing, and language standards.

In response, I reduced the assignments to one per week, reduced the questions to one per assignment, and stipulated a length of 700 words, or two typewritten pages. At the end of the semester, students' reaction to the use of TAR assignments improved more than 20 percentage points. Of 90 students, 65% said the learning was worth the work, while only 35% answered no. Despite the changes, a small number of students had become disaffected with the course. On an end-of-semester questionnaire, about six out of 90 respondents harshly criticized the TARs, with comments such as: "I HATED THEM!" and "WAY TOO MUCH WRITING!!! We have other classes too." Such feedback was helpful in making adjustments to the way I implemented JiTT the next time I taught the course.

When I taught the course again in 2008 I decided to give more assignments but drop the writing-standards and relax the length requirement. The new expectation was for students to demonstrate they had "done the readings and thought about them." After the first three rounds, except for very short responses, most students scored in the 90s. This adjustment let me assign more TARs—17 in 2008, compared with 11 in 2006—and ask two questions on each TAR assignment instead of one. I changed the weight of the TARs component from 30% to 20% of the semester grade. Finally, I explained to students repeatedly that the TARs were formative, intended to help students develop their critical thinking skills, respond deeply to photographs, and practice the mental operations that were required to perform well on their essay exams and papers. Although I was reluctant to abandon the language standards, I decided to focus the TARs solely on critical thinking, not on developing writing skills. Instead, I used the two papers assigned in the course to develop and assess students' writing skills. Support for this two-pronged approach is provided by college writing authority John Bean, who advocates using writing as a process instead of emphasizing its use as a finished product. Although he calls for professional writing at the end of the process, he encourages instructors to assign frequent, short, personal-writing assignments as the "seedbed . . . out of which committed professional writing can emerge" (Bean, 1996, p. 52).

With the decrease in pressure and deemphasis on grades, the students' acceptance of the method increased dramatically. At the end of the 2008 semester I again asked, "Did the learning you gained from the TAR assignments make them worth the work they required?" As shown in Table 10.1, over 90% of the students said that the learning was indeed worth the effort, and over 50% of the students cited TARs, either alone or in combination with other course components, as contributing the most to the learning in the course. In response to the prompt "I developed the interest and the research tools to continue studying the history of photography long after this course ends," over 88% strongly agreed or agreed, compared to just over 80% in 2006.

Students also reported strong satisfaction in their written comments on the 2008 questionnaire. Student responses included support for the oppositional readings, the discussions, and JiTT's power to compel motivation and engagement. A sample of student comments is provided below:

- Reading on both sides really helped me understand more about the topic.
- They helped me understand the material and [discussions] also made the large lecture feel much more intimate.
- They definitely motivated me to read the readings, otherwise I wouldn't have read them, and I guarantee that the TARs made others read as well.
- Even though I sometimes didn't feel like doing them, once I sat down and actually did it I was glad that I took the time.

CONCLUSION

Implementing JiTT pedagogy in my *The History of Twentieth Century Photography* course since 2004, I have found that this teaching strategy, developed initially to help students learn physics, can be successfully adapted to humanities courses. When implemented with well-chosen readings and carefully crafted questions, the method enhances students' critical thinking skills in the best liberal arts tradition. Students consistently report that the learning they gained was worth the effort required of them.

When used injudiciously, however, JiTT can overwhelm students, pushing some to reject the method and become disaffected with the course and its subject. In 2006, I learned there is an upper limit to the amount of work instructors can require without alienating some students. JiTT responses that require intensive writing work best when the writing standards are informal and the emphasis is on analyzing ideas and applying knowledge.

In my experience, JiTT works especially well when linked to Bloom's taxonomy of cognitive skills. In particular, I try to structure the questions on TAR assignments to sequentially guide the development of higher-order cognitive skills throughout the semester. In addition to developing students' critical thinking skills, I have found that JiTT also modifies students' study habits. Many students enter this course concerned about obtaining good grades rather than developing their writing or thinking skills. In particular, some of the best students expect that they can succeed simply by taking notes, highlighting the textbook, and reviewing for exams. Poor students may rely on last minute cramming, borrowing classmates' notes, and skimming the textbook before exams. JiTT helps to reduce these counterproductive habits by engaging students in brief writing and thinking processes regularly throughout the course. In turn, the TAR assignments provide valuable practice for the types of critical thinking skills needed to perform well on exams and successfully complete a course-required research paper and other writing assignments. For students, completing TAR assignments generates both a current and future return, producing additional incentive for investing effort into TARs throughout the course.

Quantitative and written responses from my students suggest that the JiTT method increases student engagement in the learning process and enhances students' motivation to learn. If stimulating readings are chosen and thoughtful and provocative questions are asked in JiTT (TAR) exercises, student learning occurs at the highest cognitive levels in Bloom's taxonomy. Such learning produces intellectual pleasure, which creates an upward spiral supporting more motivation and engagement. As one student wrote, "Learning just makes me want to learn even more!"

Finally, JiTT promotes self-autonomy in the learning process. The best JiTT exercises require students to take responsibility for their own education, in the process developing deep and durable domain and procedural knowledge. Used as a formative assessment tool, JiTT encourages students to invest time in reading, thinking, and writing. When students believe that their efforts are contributing significantly to their learning, learning becomes its own motivation. Despite the negative reaction of a few students to JiTT methods, the majority of students continue to rise to this level. Several studies, along with other chapters in this volume, demonstrate JiTT's effectiveness at promoting students' learning in the natural and social sciences. The longitudinal data I have collected in my *The History of Twentieth Century Photography* course suggest that JiTT can be effective in motivating and engaging students in the humanities as well.

Note

1. To promote the practice of writing throughout the course, I assign: two essays based on oppositional readings, a book response, a research paper, and essay questions on midterm and final exams. There are no true-false or multiple choice assessment measures on the exams. The writing assignments comprise 86.5% of the course grade;

the remaining 13.5% is based on short-answer questions on the exams. See Maier & Simkins (chapters 4 and 8) and Pace & Middendorf (chapter 9) for additional ideas on how to use JiTT exercises in writing-intensive courses.

References

Barr, R. B., & Tagg, J. (1995). From teaching to learning—A new paradigm for undergraduate education. *Change, 27*(6), 13–25.

Bean, J. C. (1996). *Engaging ideas: The professor's guide to integrating writing, critical thinking, and active learning in the classroom.* San Francisco: Jossey-Bass.

Bloom, B. S. (1956). *Taxonomy of educational objectives: The classification of educational goals.* New York: McKay.

Bransford, J. D., Brown, A. L., & Cocking, R. R. (Eds.). (2000). *How people learn: Brain, mind, experience, and school.* Washington, D.C.: National Academy Press.

Chickering, A. W. & Gamson, Z. F. (1987). Seven principles for good practice in undergraduate education. *American Association for Higher Education Bulletin, 39* (7), 3–7.

Donald, J. G. (2002). *Learning to think: Disciplinary perspectives.* San Francisco: Jossey-Bass.

Duffy, T. M., & Jonassen, D. H. (1992). *Constructivism and the technology of instruction: A conversation.* Hillsdale, NJ: Lawerence Erlbaum.

Knightley, P. (2004). *The first casualty: The war correspondent as hero and myth-maker from the Crimea to Iraq.* Baltimore: Johns Hopkins University Press.

Perry, W. G. (1970). *Forms of intellectual and ethical development in the college years: A scheme.* New York: Holt, Rinehart and Winston.

Whelan, R. (2002) "Proving that Robert Capa's "Falling Soldier" is Genuine: A Detective Story." PBS: American Masters. Retrieved from http://www.pbs.org/wnet/americanmasters/episodes/robert-capa/in-love-and-war/47/

Contributors

Mary Elizabeth Camp, Indiana University

Claude Cookman, Indiana University

Andy Gavrin, Indiana University-Purdue University Indianapolis

Laura Guertin, Penn State University/Brandywine

Mark Maier, Glendale Community College

Kathleen Marrs, Indiana University-Purdue University Indianapolis

Joan Middendorf, Indiana University

Eric Mazur, Harvard University

Gregor Novak, Indiana University-Purdue University Indianapolis/
U.S. Air Force Academy

David Pace, Indiana University

Evelyn Patterson, U.S. Air Force Academy

Scott Simkins, North Carolina A&T State University

Carol Subiño Sullivan, Indiana University

Jessica Watkins, Harvard University

Index

ALSO AVAILABLE FROM STYLUS

New Pedagogies and Practices for Teaching in Higher Education series

 Published in Association with The National Teaching and Learning Forum

Cooperative Learning in Higher Education
Across the Disciplines, Across the Academy
Edited by Barbara J. Millis

This book provides an ideal introduction for anyone contemplating using cooperative learning methods in his or her classes.

Through a series of chapters in which experienced users of cooperative learning provide concrete examples of practice in settings as varied as a developmental mathematics course at a community college to graduate courses in history and the sciences, in small, large, hybrid and online courses, the reader is introduced to major principles such as individual accountability, positive interdependence, heterogeneous teams, group processing, and social or leadership skills.

The chapters build upon and cross-reference each other, describing particular methods and activities in detail, and how and why the authors may differ about specific practices; exemplify a reflective approach to teaching; and address assessment issues.

The authors illustrate the application of cooperative learning in disciplines as varied as biology, economics, educational psychology, financial accounting, general chemistry, and literature; and in remedial, introductory, graduate, and research methods and statistics classes

Readers will find—at whatever level they teach, and whatever their discipline—that every chapter offers pedagogical gold and teaching practices that they can adapt to their needs.

FORTHCOMING

Blended Learning
Across the Disciplines, Across the Academy
Edited by Francine S. Glazer

22883 Quicksilver Drive
Sterling, VA 20166-2102   Subscribe to our e-mail alerts:www.Styluspub.com